More Holy Humor

INSPIRATIONAL WIT AND CARTOONS

MORE HOLY HUMOR

"...And here is the underground
soundproof bunker ...for the nursery."

Cal and Rose Samra

Guideposts®

CARMEL • NEW YORK 10512

For information about the Fellowship of Merry Christians and *The Joyful Noiseletter,* please call toll-free 800-877-2757 or write: FMC, P.O. Box 895, Portage, Michigan 49081-0895. Visit FMC's Web Site: HTTP://Kalamazoo.inetmi.com/cities/ KAZOO/TJNOISE/TJNOISE.HTM

This Guideposts edition is published by special arrangement with Thomas Nelson Publishers.

ISBN 0-7852-7156-2

Printed in the United States of America

To the members of
The Fellowship of Merry Christians,
with gratitude and joy.

"He who has the faith has the fun."
—G. K. Chesterton

Contents

Introduction

Four years ago, Dr. Sherwood Eliot Wirt, a consulting editor to *The Joyful Noiseletter (JN)*, wrote a delightful book, titled *The Book of Joy*, about the lives of merry-hearted Christians of all denominations through the centuries. Now 86 years young, Dr. Wirt continues to enjoy life and reflect Jesus' joy, good cheer, and wit. A long-time friend and associate of evangelist Billy Graham and the first editor of *Decision* magazine, he is also busy writing another book, *Beloved Billy*, which includes recollections of Dr. Graham, including a chapter on Graham's light side.

Dr. Wirt unearthed and passed on to *JN* the following remarks on God's joy and laughter by evangelist Paul Rader, pastor of Moody Church in Chicago back in the 1920s:

"When God chooses a man, He puts laughter into his life. God is delighted to fill the hearts of men with laughter. The anointing oil that was poured upon the head of David put laughter into David's life.

"Laughter, after all, is the surplus of life; it is a bubbling over of the emotions, a kind of spasm of exuberance, a delight of the human heart that makes the thorax cackle; something that warms the heart and delights the brain and the imagination so that men are moved to overflowing delight.

"The joy of the Lord is our strength. You may hold all kinds of theories, but does your theory lead to joy? Is there a victorious, glorious life within your heart in spite of the conditions that are roundabout?

"Whenever this anointing oil which Jesus bestows is put into your heart, you will be able to laugh. It is the oil of His presence that makes holy laughter in the life—not only in the disposition to laugh at a joke, but the ability to laugh at calamity, to laugh at death, to laugh at the victory which the devil thought he had won.

"Jesus put a real laugh into life. . . . Thus God's Spirit moves into the heart of a man and turns him right side up; 'old things are passed away; behold, all things are become new.' Now he has laughter in his soul."

Humor, like love, crosses denominational lines. Throughout the centuries, joy, humor, and laughter have been an important part of the Christian experience.

The Fellowship of Merry Christians (FMC) was organized eleven years ago by a group of Christian humorists, comedians, cartoonists, clowns, clergy, and health professionals of all denominations who wanted to bring more healing humor and laughter into the life of churches and families. As part of our ministry of humor to all God's children who need a faith-lift, the Fellowship created *The Joyful Noiseletter*, a monthly publication that features clean jokes, anecdotes, church bulletin bloopers, spoonerisms, out-of-the-mouth-of-babes quotes, inspirational humor, prayers, and uplifting Scripture passages. Over the years, thousands of readers have contributed quips and quotes and many of the Christian world's best cartoonists have contributed cartoons to *JN*.

Pastors and editors of local church bulletins and newsletters use and reprint the humor and cartoons in *JN* in their sermons and church publications. (This permission does not apply to the cartoons in this book.) And in 1994, *JN* won awards for excellence from three Christian press associations: the Evangelical Press Association, the Associated Church Press, and the Catholic Press Association.

As it has grown, FMC has become *the* source for books, cartoons, audio and video cassettes, and prints that focus on the joy, humor, and celebration in the Christian faith. Christian bookstores follow the recommendations of *JN* and FMC's catalog on new joy and humor products. (For information on how to become a FMC member, order the newsletter, or receive a catalog, call 800-877-2757.)

Associated Press religion editor David Briggs wrote in his national column that in recent years there has been an explosion of interest in religious humor, spearheaded by the FMC. More pastors are using humor in their sermons and church bulletins.

Creator of America's number-one cartoon family, "The Family Circus," Bil Keane is a charter member of FMC and *JN* consulting editor. Keane notes that when he began "The Family Circus" cartoons in the 1960s, showing kids at prayer and the family in church, some readers wrote angry letters to him for daring to use God's name in the comics. Today, Keane observes, some of the same people who scolded him now write to thank and congratulate him for bringing the Christian message to the comics pages.

In 1996, on our tenth anniversary, the Fellowship published *Holy Humor,* a book of inspirational humor and cartoons—the best of *The Joyful Noiseletter.* A Guideposts Books and Crossings Book Club selection, the book was well-received, and many folks asked us to do a sequel.

Here it is: *More Holy Humor.*

We are deeply thankful to all of the FMC members who contributed to this book. We wish we had the space to acknowledge all of them. You'll find some acknowledgments for larger contributions in the back of this book. Thank you all, and thank You, God, for all of the laughter you have brought into our lives and the lives of thousands of other folks.

It has been said that in unity there is strength. Our experience after the first eleven years of the FMC is that in unity there is also holy hilarity. We have a lot more fun together than any one of us has alone.

—*Cal and Rose Samra, Editors*

CHAPTER 1

THE LORD'S LAUGHTER

"The One whose throne is in heaven sits laughing . . ."
—*Psalm 2:4*

"Brother Helvey is here with the black box from last night's sermon to see if we can find out what went wrong."

After the church service, a pastor told a woman, "I noticed your husband walked out in the middle of my sermon. I hope I didn't say something that offended him."

"Not at all," replied the wife. "My husband has been walking in his sleep for years."

A preacher's car broke down on a country road, far away from everything but a small tavern. When he walked inside to use the phone, he saw his old friend Hank, shabbily dressed and drunk, sitting at the bar.

"Hank, what happened?" the preacher asked. "You used to be a prosperous man."

Hank told him about all the problems he had and the bad investments he had made, and asked the pastor's advice.

"Go home," the preacher said. "And when you get there, open your Bible, and put your finger down on the page. God will give you the answer."

A year later, the preacher saw Hank wearing an expensive new suit and getting into a new Mercedes. "I'm glad to see that things turned around for you," the preacher said.

"They sure have, and I owe it all to you, pastor," Hank said. "I went home, like you said, opened my Bible, put my finger down on the page, and there was the answer: Chapter 11."

—*Rev. Warren J. Keating, First Presbyterian Church, Derby, Kansas*

After the birth of their child, an Episcopal priest, wearing his clerical collar, visited his wife in the hospital. He greeted her with a hug and a kiss, and gave her another hug and a kiss when he left.

Later, the wife's roommate commented: "Gee, your pastor is sure friendlier than mine."

When the future Pope Pius XII was still a monsignor, he told this story:

A certain abbess, the head of a female monastery, insisted that the priest chaplain of the monastery kiss her hand when meeting her. He refused. The matter was referred to Rome, which gave this decision, translated from Latin: "The chaplain is not bound to kiss the abbess, but let him make merely a slight inclination of the head as to an old relic."

—*Msgr. Arthur Tonne*, **Jokes Priests Can Tell**

A preacher in our neck of the woods had just enjoyed a hearty chicken dinner at the home of one of his parishioners. Looking out the window after dinner, the preacher remarked, "That rooster of yours seems to be a mighty proud and happy bird." The host replied, "He should. His oldest son just entered the ministry."

—*Jim Reed, Cotter, Arkansas*

"It's good to be back from the youth retreat, and although I'd *like* to say I felt your prayers covering me . . ."

© 1996 Bill Frauhiger

A Baptist pastor and a Lutheran pastor were overheard discussing the different ways their churches baptized people: total immersion and sprinkling on the head.

Lutheran pastor: "Well, just how much water do you need? Up to their knees?"

Baptist pastor: "More."
Lutheran pastor: "Up to their shoulders?"
Baptist pastor: "More."
Lutheran pastor: "Up to their chin?"
Baptist pastor: "More."
Lutheran pastor: "Over their head?"
Baptist pastor: "That's right."
Lutheran pastor: "That's where we put it."
—*Ronald E. Leese, Spring Grove, Pennsylvania*

A church congregation sat enthralled while a young, very pregnant woman rose in the choir and sang, "O Lord, make haste and deliver me."
—*Rev. James A. Simpson*

"What's the difference between a terrorist and a liturgist?" asks 80-year-old humorist Fr. Tom Walsh, of Scottsdale, Arizona, a pioneer in establishing hospital humor rooms. "You can negotiate with a terrorist."

An older minister who had pastored the same church for 40 years was asked the secret of his longevity and staying power. He replied: "I stayed when they wanted me to stay; I stayed when they wanted me to leave; I stayed when I wanted to stay; I stayed when I wanted to leave."
—*James R. Swanson,* **The Pastors Confidential,** *Costa Mesa, California*

Ministerial *pride:* altar ego.
—*Fred Sevier, Sun City, Arizona*

A pastor's wife caught three small boys stealing cherries from her cherry tree. "Do you know what the Bible says about thieves?" she asked, furiously.

"Sure, ma'am," one boy answered. "'Today, thou shalt be with me in Paradise.'"

© 1996 Dennis Daniel, *Brother Blooper*

Noah's Top 10

10. Strange! We haven't seen another boat for weeks.
 9. If only I'd brought along more rhino litter!
 8. How many times around this place makes a mile?
 7. I never want to sleep in a waterbed again.
 6. I wonder what my friends are doing right now.
 5. An outboard motor would have made this more exciting!
 4. Fish for supper—again?
 3. Does anyone have more Dramamine?
 2. What? You don't have film to photograph the rainbow?
 1. I should have killed those darn mosquitoes when I had the chance!

—*Pastor Paul W. Kummer, Grace Lutheran Church, Destin, Florida*

A lady approached the clerk in a hardware store and ordered one box of spiders and a box of cockroaches. When the clerk asked the lady why she wanted them, the lady answered: "I am the pastor's wife from the church down the street. Last night they voted my husband out of the church, and they told us when we left to leave the parsonage *exactly* as we found it.

—*Rev. James R. Swanson*

A group of teenagers met an old pastor with a white beard and decided it would be fun to tease him. "Good morning, Father Abraham," one said, bowing.

"Good morning, Father Isaac," said another teenager, also bowing.

"Good morning, Father Jacob," said a third.

Smiling, the old pastor replied: "I am neither Abraham, Isaac, nor Jacob. I am Saul, and I am looking for my father's asses. I think I have found what I am looking for."

—*Rev. Dennis R. Fakes, Lindsborg, Kansas*

After a worship service, a preacher announced: "The class on prophecy has been canceled due to unforeseen circumstances."

—*George Goldtrap, Madison, Tennessee*

On an African safari, a missionary asked the guide if it were true that a jungle animal will not attack you if you are carrying a torch.

"Well," the guide responded thoughtfully, "it depends on how fast you are carrying the torch."

While Fr. James M. Gilligan, MM, was preaching in the chapel of St. Benedict Hospital in Pusan, Korea, a woman in the congregation began to cough loudly and often. The priest said to a nun who was sitting up front, "Give that lady a glass of water!"

Then Fr. Gilligan returned to his sermon, but lost his train of thought. "Now, what was I saying?" he murmured.

The nun replied, "Give that lady a glass of water!"

—**Maryknoll** *magazine*

I love a finished speaker,
I really, really do.
I don't mean one who's polished.
I just mean one who's through.
— *Rev. Bernard Brunsting*

A pastor joined a local service club where some of his congregation were also members. Assigned the task of making name tags for the group, the members of his congregation decided to play a practical joke on the pastor, and labeled his tag Hog Caller.

When the pastor saw his name tag, he laughed. "They usually call me the Shepherd of the Sheep," he quipped, "but I suppose our members know themselves better than I do."
— *Rev. Dennis R. Fakes*

"I love California! Tremors give me a lot of great sermon ideas about the instability of the world."

A Lutheran pastor who served a deaf congregation fumbled through his sermons weekly. Although he had a good background in sign language, the pastor didn't know the sign for "testament." So every time he referred to a Scripture verse, he had to spell out the word *Old* or *New* and then the word *Testament*.

One Sunday morning the pastor got creative and invented a sign for the missing word. When he read from the Psalms, he signed "Old" and then made the sign for the letter T. The congregation giggled. Then, when he read from Luke, he signed "New" and did the same T sign. Again, the congregation giggled.

After the service, some of the parishioners were still giggling as they greeted the pastor. Finally, a member told him: "Do you know what you read today? You read lessons from the old and new toilet."

—FMC member Ronald Leese, Spring Grove, Pennsylvania

A Presbyterian minister carefully prepared his sermons, word-for-word, and placed them in a loose-leaf binder, which he took with him to the pulpit Sunday mornings. One Saturday night, his son, just for fun, removed a sheet from the scripted sermon.

As the preacher read his sermon the next morning—"and Adam said to Eve"—he turned the page and discovered it was missing. Perplexed, he looked at the congregation and exclaimed, "There must be a leaf missing here."

—Humorist Carroll Lamb

The pope came to New York City and hailed a cab from the airport to St. Patrick's Church. Because he was running late, the pope asked the cabby to speed it up, but the cabby refused. Finally, the frustrated pope demanded that the cabby pull over and let him drive.

No sooner had the cabby given in to the pope's wish than a policeman stopped them. When the officer looked inside the cab, his eyes widened, and he ran back to his car to call the police chief.

"I've stopped a speeding cab, but there's someone very important inside," he told the chief. "What do I do?"

"Give the driver a ticket," the chief growled.

"But he's got a very important passenger."

"Well, who is it?" the chief asked. "The mayor? The governor? The President?"

"I don't know," the officer replied. "But the pope is driving him."

—*Mrs. Harriet Adams, Morton, Pennsylvania*

A pastor went on a week's vacation and left his new young associate pastor in charge of the Sunday service. When he returned, he asked a member how his associate had performed.

"He gave a dull sermon—not much in it," the member answered.

When he saw his associate, the pastor asked how he had felt about Sunday morning.

"Very good," the associate responded. "I didn't have time to put together a sermon, but I found one of yours. So I preached it."

"Come in, Reverend . . . er . . . ah . . . I don't remember your name, but I never forget a face."

The son of a poor widow struck it rich in the stock market. Wanting to show his love for his mother, he went to a pet shop and asked the owner for the rarest and most expensive pet in his shop.

The owner said he had a rare parrot, worth $50,000, which could recite the Ten Commandments and other Scripture verses.

No gift was too costly for his beloved mother, the son decided. So he bought the bird and shipped it to her.

The next day, he called his mother. "Did you get the bird?" he asked.

"I sure did, son," she replied. "Thank you, it was delicious!"

—*Rev. Dennis R. Fakes*

© 1996 Doc Goodwin

When a church seeks a pastor, they want the strength of an eagle, the grace of a swan, the gentleness of a dove, the friendliness of a sparrow, and the night hours of an owl. And when they catch that bird, they expect the pastor to live on the food of a canary.

—*Anonymous*

A man went to a church several times during the week in an effort to see the preacher, but the preacher was never there. Finally, he ran into the church janitor and inquired: "Your preacher isn't here much, is he?"

The janitor replied: "No, sir, and he's not much when he is here."

—*Sarah Nugent, Brentwood, Tennessee*

"I used to be a street preacher. Now, I'm an interactive superhighway info-minister."

© 1996 Jonny Hawkins

"There is no better Christian humorist on land or sea," Grady Wilson said of the late Baptist pastor Tal Bonham. Bonham served as executive director of the State Convention of Baptists in Ohio for many years. A charter member of the Fellowship of Merry Christians and a consulting editor to The Joyful Noiseletter, *Bonham left his audiences howling.*

A pastor was talking with a hard-working woman who was a devoted member, present at all services. He expressed his thanks for seeing her so attentive to the services every Sunday.

"Yes," she said. "It is such a rest after a long, hard week's work to come to church, sit down on the soft cushions, and not think about anything."

— *Tal Bonham*

A young man was asked to preach at a camp meeting just before the Sunday morning service. As hundreds of people began gathering on the grounds, the young preacher panicked and ran into the bishop's tent. "What shall I do, bishop?" he implored. "They've asked me to preach, but I don't have any sermon."

"Trust the Lord, young man," the bishop advised with great dignity. "Just trust the Lord." Then, the bishop marched out of his tent.

Frustrated, the young man picked up the bishop's Bible and flipped through it, hoping to find an inspiring verse. Instead, he found some typewritten sermon notes he liked very much. So he took the bishop's Bible and notes and went to the service.

The young preacher amazed everyone with his sermon, and the people crowded around him after the service. Suddenly, the bishop pushed his way through the crowd.

"Young man," the bishop thundered. "You preached the sermon I was going to preach tonight! Now what am I going to do?"

"Trust the Lord, bishop," the young man replied. "Just trust the Lord."

— *Tal Bonham,* **Treasury of Clean Church Jokes**

The pastor confronted his tipsy church member: "Joe, whiskey is your worst enemy."

"But didn't you tell us last Sunday to love our enemies?" Joe replied.

"Sure," the pastor answered, "but I didn't say anything about swallowing them."

— *Southeastern Oil Review*

Pastors, of course, are not supposed to curse. Instead of cursing, one pastor I know, when he's alone, calls out the names of several members of his congregation—with feeling.

— *Rev. Dennis R. Fakes*

Entertaining an audience in Sturgis, Michigan, comedian Steve Allen mentioned that some of his friends have been writing books on reincarnation lately. Of one of the authors, he observed, "I've known her since she was a cocker spaniel."

HEAVENLY HUMOR

"Don't get me wrong—I love it here. It's just that I'm a little disappointed about the harp thing being a myth."

© 1992 Ed Sullivan

In the middle of a long-winded sermon, a small child was overheard asking his mother in a whisper that was heard for pews around: "Mommy, are you sure this is the only way we can get to heaven?"

When the new preacher moved into town, one of the first people he met said, "I certainly hope that you're not one of these narrow-minded ministers who think that only the members of their congregation are going to heaven."

"I'm even more narrow-minded than that," replied the preacher. "I'm pretty sure that some of the members of my congregation *aren't* going to make it."

—*Msgr. Arthur Tonne*

A minister and a bus driver reached the Pearly Gates together and were assigned their quarters. The minister got a dilapidated shack in a farm meadow; the bus driver, a home in an elegant neighborhood.

The pastor went to St. Peter and said, "While on earth I preached to thousands of people and tried hard to follow all the commandments. What an exemplary life the bus driver must have led!"

St. Peter responded, "During your sermons, most everybody slept, but when the bus driver worked, everybody prayed."

—*Rev. Dr. James L. White, Christ Church, Rockville, Maryland*

When Sherlock Holmes, the great detective, arrived in heaven, St. Peter said to him: "Can you help us solve a mystery? You see, Adam and Eve have been missing for the past several thousand years. Can you find them for us?"

Sherlock began his investigation, and after several days, he returned and told St. Peter: "You will find Adam and Eve over there beyond the gate." He pointed them out.

"How did you find them?" St. Peter asked.

"Elementary, my dear St. Peter," Sherlock replied. "They are the only two up here who have no navels."

—*Rev. Dennis R. Fakes, Lindsborg, Kansas*

A pastor adjusted his height and knelt in front of a group of church preschoolers at a special service. He talked to the children about being good and going to heaven. At the end of his talk, the pastor asked, "Where do you want to go?"

The little voices shouted out, "Heaven!"
"And what must you be to get to heaven?" the pastor asked.
"Dead!" a loud chorus yelled.
—*Msgr. Arthur Tonne*

The Family Circus

Reprinted with permission of Bil Keane

ERMA WOULD HAVE LAUGHED AT HER TEN MALE PALLBEARERS

Shortly after humorist Erma Bombeck died of kidney failure, April 22, 1996, cartoonist Bil Keane, her longtime friend and neighbor in Paradise Valley, Arizona, drew a special *Family Circus* cartoon (above). A tribute by Keane also appeared on the brochure for Bombeck's funeral mass at St. Thomas the Apostle Church, attended by 1,200 people who cried and laughed at recollections of her.

Bombeck once wrote a column about heaven in which she speculated that "it's probably just one big *Jeopardy!* game in the sky, where all day long you struggle to remember names."

Keane, a pallbearer, commented after the funeral: "I'm sure Erma would find it laughable that, after all her columns about losing weight, they needed ten men to carry her casket."

Bombeck, who was married to the same man, Bill Bombeck, for almost 50 years, brought laughter to millions with her newspaper and magazine columns and books.

Keane once paid this tribute to her: "My friends Erma Bombeck and Art Buchwald have done far more for the health of humanity than Madame Curie or Dr. Christiaan Barnard."

Humorist Art Buchwald commented, "She brought joy to an awful lot of people."

"Most of my readers are housewives," Bombeck once wrote. "we're all in this mess together. Let's get some fun out of it."

The Family Circus

"Heaven is a great big hug that lasts forever."

Reprinted with permission of Bil Keane

"Up here it certainly is easy to tell if people are left- or right-wingers."

FMC member Fr. Tom Walsh also had befriended Bombeck when he was at St. Thomas the Apostle Church. Fourteen years ago, Walsh, who was then teaching a course called "Humor, Hilarity, Healing, and Happy Hypothalami," asked Bombeck if she thought humor is healing. Bombeck replied with a delightful letter. Here's an excerpt from the letter:

Dear Father Tom:

I suspect you have me confused with Norman Cousins. He's several inches taller, and he laughed his way through illness. He got a best-seller out of his illness. I got three children. Those are the breaks.

I am a great believer in your premise that humor heals. I have nothing to back it up physically, but I have file drawers of pure testimonials.

I've had pitiful letters from people who swear they don't have a sense of humor and want to know how to develop one, because they've heard how much of a stabilizer one is. And they're right.

What I have been doing for 16 years in my column is to put my life in perspective, the frustration of raising children, the loneliness, the pain, and the futility of it all. And it works.

Good luck. I miss you a lot at St. Thomas. Was it something I said?

Millions of us are going to miss Erma Bombeck.

"Perhaps it's more than just a coincidence that we've all never been audited by the IRS."

FUNEREAL HUMOR

"I'LL TAKE HEAVEN"

... by golly

MAN, MAN, MAGNIFICENT MAN—

CREATES FORCES THAT OUTSHINE THE STARS.

HE CAN SHOOT HIMSELF UP and TAP DANCE ON THE MOON

OR HURL HIMSELF CLEAR OUT TO MARS!

HE CAN UNLEASH A FORCE THAT EVAPORATES STEEL,

SINCE HE'S LEARNED HOW AN ATOM BEHAVES.

YET HE HAS NO RECOURSE BUT TO BOW TO THE FORCE.

THAT SUMMONS THE DEAD FROM THEIR GRAVES.

As he preached a funeral service about the resurrection one afternoon, the minister couldn't seem to find a stopping place. The funeral director grew concerned about the time and stepped over to a church member. "Does your pastor always speak this long at funerals," he whispered.

"That's a fine sermon, isn't it?" the gentleman replied, nodding.

Somewhat embarrassed, the funeral director agreed, but he continued to look at his watch every few minutes. After a while, the church member tugged at his sleeves.

"What's the matter?" he demanded. "Don't you believe in the resurrection?"

"I sure do," the funeral director answered. "But I'm afraid we won't get this man buried in time for it."

—*Tal Bonham,* **Treasury of Clean Church Jokes**

The funeral of the composer of the "hokey pokey" dance was very hard on those who attended. They'd put his right leg in, he'd put his right leg out; they'd put his right leg in . . .

—*FMC member Rev. Stuart A. Schlegel, Santa Cruz, California*

TOMBSTONE HUMOR

Remember, man who passes by,
As you are now,
So once was I,
And as I am now, so must you be.
Prepare yourself to follow me.

Beneath the epitaph, a living wit wrote:

To follow you, I'm not content,
Until I learn which way you went.

—*Catherine Hall, Pittsburgh, Pennsylvania*

When an elderly spinster died, her family could not come up with a suitable epitaph for her gravestone until one of the family remembered that a cousin was a sportswriter and asked him to compose the inscription. He wrote:

Here lie the bones of Mary Jones
Her life it knew no terrors.
Born an old maid, died an old maid
No runs, no hits, no errors.

—*FMC member Donald D. Kaynor,*
  Battle Creek, Michigan

On the gravestone of an Archbishop Potter:

A lack and well-a-day
Potter himself
Is turned to clay.

H ere lie the bones
of Alfred Jones.
When from the tomb
to meet his doom
he rises amidst sinners,
take him to dwell
in heaven or hell,
whichever serves big dinners.

H ere lies the body
of Mary Gwynne
who was so very pure within.
She cracked the shell
of her earthly skin and hatched herself
a cherubim.

On the gravestone of a 19th-century quack doctor:

R eader, Dr. Johnson is, alas, no more
He visits those he visited before.
   —JN *consulting editor Paul Thigpen,*
      Springfield, Missouri

S even wives I've buried
with as many
a fervent prayer;
If we all should meet in heaven,
won't there be
trouble there?

Here lies the preacher,
judge, and poet Peter,
who broke the laws
of God and man
and meter.

"No ma'am, we don't do memorial services
for dogs. What? $75, you say? Well, why
didn't you say Fritz was of our religious
persuasion?"

© 1996 Dennis Daniel, *Brother Blooper*

Matilda Graham
has gone to rest
she now reclines
on Abraham's breast
Peace at last for Matilda Graham
but not for Father Abraham.

On the gravestone of a Wal-Mart shopper:

Gone to Wal·Mart.

Before he died at the age of 100, a reporter asked comedian George Burns what he would like on his epitaph. "I'd like to be standing there reading it," Burns replied.

Two things are inevitable: death and taxes. It's just too bad they don't come in that order. This year I'm using the new IRS 1040 EZ form. It has only three lines·
    Line A: How much did you make last year?
    Line B: How much do you have left?
    Line C: Send B.
    —JN consulting editor Steve Feldman, Jefferson City, Missouri

When Pope John XXIII was dying, Cardinal Testa came to see him and asked: "How is my friend, Roncalli?"
    The pope answered with great effort: "Your friend Roncalli is really bad, but I heard on the radio that John XXIII is much better."
    —Fr. Eugene M. Rooney, SJ, Montevideo, Uruguay

A florist's new assistant took a telephone order from a customer. "The ribbon must be white," said the woman on the phone, "with gold letters reading 'Rest in Peace' on both sides. And, if you can squeeze it in, 'We Shall Meet in Heaven.'"
    When the floral tribute reached the home of the deceased, the inscription read: REST IN PEACE ON BOTH SIDES! IF YOU CAN SQUEEZE IN, WE SHALL MEET IN HEAVEN!
    —Liguorian

A zealous man once telephoned Woodrow Wilson in the wee hours of the morning when Wilson was governor of New Jersey, rousing him from sleep. "Governor Wilson," the man announced, "your commissioner of highways just died, and I would like to take his place."
    "If it's all right with the undertaker, it's all right with me," Wilson replied.
    —Pastor Viggo Aronsen, Kerrville, Texas

Minnie Pearl, "The First Lady of Comedy" in country circles, went to the Lord March 4, 1996, at the age of 83. Although she aspired to be a Shakespearean actress as a young woman, she said she "soon found out that God wanted me to be a comedienne."

One of her standard lines: *"Laughter is God's hand on the shoulders of a troubled world."* Another favorite: *"There will be no male pallbearers at my funeral. If they won't take me out when I'm alive, I won't let them take me out when I'm dead."*

"When Minnie arrives in heaven," observed *JN* consulting editor George Goldtrap, who was a friend of Pearl's, "I'm sure she'll say, *'Howdeeeeeeeeeee! I'm just so proud to be here!'*"

If we expire when we die, shouldn't we inspire while we live?
—*George Goldtrap*

CHAPTER
4

YOU MIGHT BE A PREACHER IF . . .

You Might Be a Preacher If . . .

1. You hesitate to tell people what you do for a living.
2. You've ever dreamed you were preaching only to awaken and discover you were.
3. You've ever wondered why people couldn't die at more appropriate times.
4. You find yourself counting people at a sporting event.
5. You're leading the church into the 21st century, but you don't know what you're preaching on Sunday.
6. A church picnic is no picnic.
7. You jiggle all the commode handles at the church before you leave.
8. You've ever spoken for free and were worth every penny of it.
9. You drive a Buick with more than 100,000 miles on it.
10. People sleep while you're talking.
11. It's Sunday, but Monday's coming.
12. You feel guilty when you go fishing.
13. Instead of getting "ticked off," you get "grieved in your spirit."
14. You've ever been tempted to take an offering at a family reunion.
15. You read sermons to your kids at night instead of bedtime stories.

16. You'd rather talk to people with every head bowed and every eye closed.
17. You've ever wanted to "lay hands" on a deacon's neck.
18. You often feel like you're herding mules rather than shepherding sheep.
19. Your greatest joys have been in the church.

—*Reprinted with permission from* **You Might Be a Preacher If . . .** ,
by FMC member Stan Toler and Mark Hollingsworth,
long-time pastors in Oklahoma (Tulsa, Oklahoma:
Albury Publishing, © *1995).*

"Well, if you don't believe in the organized church, you'll love ours—we're as disorganized as they come!"

© 1991 Dennis Daniel, *Brother Blooper*

You can always identify the pastor of any parish. He's the one who goes around turning out the lights.

Two young priests were discussing how frugal their senior pastor was. Said one: "When he dies, if he sees light at the end of the tunnel, he'll put it out."

—*Msgr. Charles Dollen,* **The Priest,** *Poway, California*

You May Be Headed for Termination If . . .

1. The leadership of the church continually talks to you about playing ball with them.
2. You become ill and ask the deacons to pray for you; they vote on praying for you, and it passes by a vote of 12 to 10.
3. Your reserved parking spot is now marked Quest Parking.
4. While you were on vacation, the lock on your study door was changed and the staff refuses to give you the new key.
5. Everyone stops talking when you enter the room.
6. You were not invited to the staff Christmas party.
7. The chairman of the personnel committee gives you a freshly painted sign to wear: Will Preach for Food.
8. The new business cards which the church provided for you have a place to pencil in the name of the pastor.
9. The chairman of the deacons asks you for a recent résumé.
10. The church has a leadership appreciation service and doesn't recognize you.

—*Will Pollard, editor,* **Ohio Baptist Messenger,** *Columbus, Ohio*

CHAPTER 5

ALL THE DAYS OF HER LIFE

One month before our son Matthew was born, I was sent home from work by my doctor. She said, "Liz, you have got to get those ankles up in the air!" Not straight up, you understand, but elevated above my hips so the swelling would go down—a necessary move, because my ankles did look ridiculous. "Squisshh! Squisshh!" they went when I walked. I couldn't wear open-toed shoes, or the water ran out.

So there I was one afternoon in my ninth month, dutifully keeping my ankles up as I sat in an overstuffed chair and chatted on the phone with my friend Debra. In the laundry room a few feet away, I'd just put in a load of clothes. The washer was sounding unusually loud, and I knew I should put the phone down and check on it, but that would've required getting out of the chair, a seven-minute ordeal of huffing and puffing.

Instead, I reached over and shut the door to the laundry room and kept right on talking—for an hour. (This is not difficult for me.)

When I finally hung up the phone, I knew something was very wrong because the washer was still running. Even on the longest cycle, it doesn't go an hour. I struggled out of the chair, made my way to the laundry room, and opened the door.

It was not a pretty sight. The washer hose was loose and spraying hot water everywhere, as it had been for an hour. The walls, the curtains, the ironing board, the piles of clean laundry: *Everything* was dripping wet. But that's not all.

This laundry room had a hardwood floor, so the water had also gone through the cracks and down through the subfloor and right into my husband's basement office. That was the same office where he had, days earlier, gotten organized for the first time in our short married life and put up nice neat shelves with all his books and papers.

Afraid to look, but knowing I had to, I waddled to the top of the basement steps and peered down. Just as I had feared, all his books and papers were floating around about the second step.

Of course, I had to call him. "Bill!" I wailed into the telephone, summoning all my prenatal hysteria for a sympathy vote, "Bill! There's . . . there's water everywhere!"

He almost shouted into the phone. "I'll meet you at the hospital in five minutes!"

"All right, the motion to call a plumber passes, four to two."

In her book, Reflecting His Image *(Thomas Nelson), Liz Curtis Higgs observes:*

The Latin word *disciplere* means "one who learns by doing." Doing, eh? No wonder I struggle in my Christian walk. I'm trying to learn by *sitting!* Sitting in Sunday school, sitting in church, sitting at fellowship suppers. . . . This discipleship stuff is hard work!

Eve and I

When I get to Heaven,
I'm gonna look for Eve;
I have one major question
That really makes me grieve.
I want to ask that woman
Exactly why she ate
Forbidden fruit from Satan . . .
Was she too hungry to wait?

It seems that God provided
Food beyond belief;
So what in the world made her listen
To the words of the liar-thief?

When the tempter first started speaking,
I think, my dearest madam,
If you had only said to him,
"Let me check this out with Adam,"
We women would have peace and quiet
Instead of receiving the blame
For every sinful action
That takes place on the human plane!

I'm really upset with this female
And I'd like to tell her so;
But I must admit I'm so like her
As off to the candy store I go!

—*"Mary the Overeater" Wright McHarris, Knoxville, Tennessee*

An elderly woman in a nursing home declined her pastor's suggestion that she get a hearing aid. "At 91, I've heard enough," she said.

—*Catherine Hall, Pittsburgh, Pennsylvania*

"This is a sermon on death, Emily—stop thinking about the kids going back to school."

FMC member Rev. Gordon McLean, director of the Juvenile Justice Ministry, Metro Chicago Youth for Christ, says he met some interesting neighbors when he moved to a new apartment complex in the Chicago area. One woman told him, "I miss my ex-husband, but my aim is getting better." Another woman said, "Sometimes I wake up grumpy, but most of the time I just let him sleep."

OUT OF THE MOUTHS OF BABES

A little girl became restless as the preacher's sermon dragged on and on. Finally, she leaned over to her mother and whispered, "Mommy, if we give him the money now, will he let us go?"

—*Jim Reed, Cotter, Arkansas*

"Dad," a little boy asked, "Did you go to Sunday school every week?"

"I sure did, son," his father replied.

"I'll bet it won't do me any good, either," the boy said.

—*Rev. Dennis R. Fakes, Lindsborg, Kansas*

A mother was watching her four-year-old child playing outside in a small plastic pool half filled with water. He was happily walking back and forth across the pool, making big splashes. Suddenly, he stopped, stepped out of the pool, and began to scoop water out of the pool with a pail.

"Why are you pouring the water out, Johnny?" the mother asked.

"'Cause my teacher said Jesus walked on water. And this water won't work," the boy replied.

—*Rev. Woody McKay, Stone Mountain, Georgia*

A Sunday school teacher asked a little boy: "Bobby, do you believe in the devil?"

The Family Circus

"We asked God to bless this LAST night!"

"No," the boy said. "He's just like Santa Claus. I think it's my daddy."

A boy was watching his father, a pastor, write a sermon. "How do you know what to say?" he asked.

"Why, God tells me," the clergyman replied.

"Oh," said the lad. "Then why do you keep crossing things out?"
—*Archbishop John L. May, St. Louis, Missouri*

When JN *consulting editor Andy Fisher visited Ireland, Maurice Kavanagh, a parishioner at the Cathedral of the Holy Trinity in Waterford, told him this story:*

After mass, a little Catholic girl told her mother, "I can't wait to get to heaven because they have such beautiful clothes there."

"Honey, where did you get that idea?" the mother asked.

The little girl, recalling a special prayer called the "Memorare" at the end of the rosary, replied: "Mommy, remember when we pray 'To thee do we send up our size (sighs).'"

The Family Circus

"Can we talk?"

Reprinted with permission of Bil Keane

Country singer Barbara Mandrell said that when her son Nathan was born, she always sang three songs to him: "Jesus Loves Me," "This Is the Day the Lord Has Made," and "Jesus Loves the Little Children." She said: "I wondered which of these would be the first song that Nathan would sing on his own. It was none of those three. The first song he sang was 'All My Ex's Live in Texas.'"
  —**The Detroit News**

Our daughter was reading about Adam and Eve to her five-year-old son, Sean, from a child's book of Bible stories. When she came to the part where the Lord asked Adam why he'd eaten the apple and

Adam blamed the woman in the garden, Sean exclaimed "Oh, so he was the first tattletale!"

—*K. T. Gundersen, Simsbury, Connecticut*

A father took his five-year-old son to several baseball games where "The Star-Spangled Banner" was sung before the start of the game. Then the father and son attended a church on a Sunday shortly before Independence Day. The congregation sang "The Star-Spangled Banner"; and after everyone sat down, the boy suddenly yelled out: "Play ball!"

—*Jean Spencer, Camarillo, California*

Rev. Dan Yeary of the North Phoenix Baptist Church in Arizona recently quoted a five-year-old's version of John 3:16:

"For God so loved the world that He gave His only begotten Son, that whosoever believeth in Him should not perish, but have ever-laughing life."

En route with the family to church, a five-year-old boy was told that this would be a special day because a neighbor's baby girl, Brenda, was to be blessed.

The little boy was looking forward to the occasion, but fell asleep during the service. When he awoke, he told his mother, "I'm sorry. I fell asleep and missed Brenda getting blasted!"

—*Jean W. Spencer, Camarillo, California*

I took my three-year-old granddaughter, Denise, to my church's Thanksgiving celebration. Cans and boxes of food and pumpkins were stacked around the altar, and I explained to Denise that the food was for poor people who didn't have enough to eat.

When the choir began to process toward the altar, Denise cried out: "Look Grandma! Here come the poor people now!"

—*Shirley Thomsen, Vancouver, Washington*

While in church, a father whispered to his daughter that she should be quiet because they were in God's house. The girl looked all around the church, and asked her father, "Which door will God be coming in?"

—*Jean Spencer*

A Sunday school teacher asked her class, "Does anyone here know what we mean by sins of omission?"

A small girl replied: "Aren't those the sins we should have committed, but didn't?"

—*Catherine Hall*

A six-year-old boy was overheard reciting the Lord's Prayer at a church service: "And forgive us our trash passes as we forgive those who pass trash against us."

A small boy told a Sunday school teacher: "When you die, God takes care of you like your parents did when you were alive—only God doesn't yell at you all the time."

—*Rev. Dennis R. Fakes*

After a Vacation Bible School teacher read the story of the prodigal son, she asked, "What does it mean to 'waste your substance on riotous living?'"

Seven-year-old Tim spoke up: "It means to spend all your money on bubble gum."

After a local service club president introduced the speaker, a minister, with a lengthy, complimentary account of his accomplishments, the minister's daughter, seated in the front row, turned to her mother and asked: "I thought Dad was going to speak."

—*Rev. Bernard Brunsting, Stuart, Florida*

"C'Mon, Dad, raise your hands! You're not in church!"

A five-year-old boy was explaining the story of the fallen angels to his even younger sister:

"One day up in heaven God said to the angels, 'Pick up your toys.' Some angels said, 'We won't.' And so God started hell."

—Msgr. Arthur Tonne

My wife was reading our two-year-old son, Elijah, the story of the Good Samaritan at bedtime. She got to the place where the lawyer challenged Jesus with a question. "And who is my neighbor?" My wife read the lawyer's question.

"I know!" said Elijah. "Mr. Rogers!"

—Paul Thigpen

After church on Sunday morning, a young boy suddenly announced to his mother, "Mom, I've decided I'm going to be a minister when I grow up."

"That's okay with us," the mother said, "but what made you decide to be a minister?"

"Well," the boy said, "I'll have to go to church on Sunday anyway, and I figure it will be more fun to stand up and yell than to sit still and listen."

—George Goldtrap, Madison, Tennessee

A heavy snowstorm closed the schools in one town. When the children returned to school a few days later, one grade-school teacher asked her students whether they had used the time away from school constructively.

"I sure did, teacher," one little girl replied. "I just prayed for more snow."

—*Catherine Hall*

© 1996 Doc Goodwin, *Phillip's Flock*

On Ash Wednesday, congregants at Kilbourne (Ohio) United Methodist Church were coming forward for the imposition of ashes on their foreheads. Two-year-old Brenna Wagoner, upset that her mother was not taking her to the altar, was overheard exclaiming: "But I want to get a tattoo just like Daddy's!"

—*Rev. Donna J. van Trees, Kilbourne, Ohio*

A four-year-old Catholic boy was playing with a four-year-old Protestant girl in a children's pool in the backyard. They splashed each other, got very wet, and decided to take their wet clothes off. The little boy looked at the little girl and said, "Golly, I didn't know there was that much difference between Catholics and Protestants."

—*Jean Spencer*

Three small boys were bragging about their fathers. The first boasted that his dad owned a farm. The second said his dad owned a factory. The third boy, a pastor's son, replied: "That's nothin'. My dad owns hell."

"No way," another boy scoffed. "How can a man own hell?"

"Sure he can," the preacher's son said. "My mom told my grandma that the elders of our church gave it to him last night."

On vacation with her family in Montana, a mother drove her van past a church in a small town and pointing to it, told the children that it was St. Francis' Church. "It must be a franchise," her eight-year-old son said. "We've got one of those in our town too."

A Sunday school teacher challenged her children to take some time on Sunday afternoon to write a letter to God. They were to bring back their letter the following Sunday. One little boy wrote: "Dear God, We had a good time at church today. Wish You could have been there."

—*Rev. Richard L. Hadfield, Plainfield (Pennsylvania) Lutheran Church*

FMC member Fr. Michael Hayduk, pastor of St. Mary's Byzantine Catholic Church in Cleveland, Ohio, visited the church's preschool and day-care center one day. A new group of little ones had started at the center, and one boy, about three years old, asked the priest, "Why do you dress funny?"

Fr. Hayduk told him he was a priest and this was the uniform that priests wear. Then the boy pointed to Hayduk's collar insert and asked: "Does that hurt? Do you have a boo-boo there?"

Hayduk took the plastic collar insert out and showed it to the boy. The name of the manufacturer is embossed on the reverse side. The boy felt the letters, and the priest asked him, "Do you know what those words say?"

"Yes, I do!" said the boy, who was not old enough to read. "It says, 'Kills ticks and fleas up to six months!'"

Bouncing out of her first day in nursery school at Mount Moriah Presbyterian Church in Port Henry, New York, a three-year-old girl gleefully informed her mother: "We had juice and Billy Graham crackers!"

—*Rev. Bob White*

Rev. David A. Stammerjohn, pastor of Laboratory Presbyterian Church, Washington, Pennsylvania, spent a week at the Synod school with his two children. The school's theme focused on Moses and the Exodus. When they returned home, his five-year-old daughter excitedly greeted her mother: "Guess what, Mommy. We made unleaded bread!"

After Sunday school, FMC member Elsie Huber of Huntington, New York, asked her son what he had learned. "In Him we live and move and have our beans," the boy replied.

The old pastor made it a practice to visit the parish school one day a week. He walked into the fourth-grade class, where the children were studying the states, and asked them how many states they could name. They came up with about 40 names. He jokingly told them that in his day students knew the names of all the states.

One lad raised his hand and said, "Yes, but in those days there were only 13."

—*Msgr. Charles Dollen,* **The Priest**

A mother overheard her little girl praying:

"Now I lay me down to rest.
I pray I pass tomorrow's test.
If I should die before I wake,
That's one less test I'll have to take."

—*George Goldtrap*

The Family Circus

"Be quiet, Jeffy, or you'll be sent
to God's office."

Four-year-old Tucker Jones attended Vacation Bible School at our church. The theme was "Discipleship and Saving Mother Earth." His mother, Trish Jones, asked Tucker what he had learned. He immediately told her all about "Jesus and the 12 recycles."
—*Rev. Larry Wilkinson, First United Methodist Church, Gastonia, North Carolina*

My five-year-old grandson, Daniel Meredith, was taken to church for the first time. On the way home, he asked, "If that is God's house, how come there are cracks in the ceiling?"
—*John H. Hirsh, M.D., Ft. Lauderdale, Florida*

After listening restlessly to a long and tedious sermon, a six-year-old boy asked his father what the preacher did the rest of the week.

"Oh, he's a very busy man," the father replied. "He takes care of church business, visits the sick, ministers to the poor. . . . And then he has to have time to rest up. Talking in public isn't an easy job, you know."

The boy thought about that, then said: "Well, listening ain't easy, either."

—*Msgr. Arthur Tonne,* **Jokes Priests Can Tell**

A little boy went to dine with his parents at the home of an elderly gentleman. After watching the old man bow his head and speak in a soft voice, the boy asked his mother: "What did Mr. Bryan say to his plate?"

—*Dick Van Dyke*

FMC member Pastor Gerald Krum of St. John Lutheran Church, Lewistown, Pennsylvania, has a game plan for his children's sermons. A child brings up a box in which there is something the pastor has not seen. Krum must create a message on what he finds in the box.

One Sunday morning, Patrick presented the pastor with a box with a portable phone inside.

"We have six members in the hospital now," the pastor began. "I think I'll call God and ask him to help them get better. Now what is His number? I'll try 437-2156." After he dialed the number, he said, "No, that's not it. What should I dial next?"

"Try 911," little Alex answered.

The pupils at Cheam School, one of the most respected boys' schools in England, were being briefed for the expected visit the next day of Lord Geoffrey Fisher, the Archbishop of Canterbury. They were told, "If the archbishop speaks to you, you must address him as either 'My Lord' or 'Your Grace.'"

When the distinguished cleric arrived complete with gaiters, the boys were marshaled in a row, shoes shined and cheeks scrubbed. The archbishop walked along the line smiling and stopped to speak to one boy. "How old are you, sonny?" he asked.

The boy spoke up: "My God, I'm ten!"

—*Sherwood Eliot Wirt,* **The Book of Joy**

An elderly couple took their four-year-old grandson to church on Sunday morning. The grandmother was a choir member, and she told the boy that he would be sitting with his grandfather in the church. She took the boy aside, gave him a quarter, and instructed him to poke his grandfather now and then to keep him awake during the service.

Grandpa slept through much of the service, and after church, grandma asked the boy why he hadn't followed her instructions. The boy replied: "Grandpa gave me 50 cents not to wake him."

—*Catherine Hall*

FMC member John Burkhalter of Roswell, Georgia, decided to teach his two young boys how to use a concordance. As they grow, he explained, he "wanted them to be able to look up Scripture that talks to the topic they are struggling with at the time."

Dad began by setting out both the family's large Bible and the large concordance on the table. He then asked the boys: "You know what the Bible is, but do you know what the concordance is?"

Eight-year-old Paul answered, "Is it the sequel?"

A Jewish boy in grade school was listening to his Hebrew teacher quoting Scripture. "The Lord our God is One," the teacher declared.

"When will He be two?" the youngster asked.

—*Andy Fisher, Denville, New Jersey*

JN associate editor Rose Samra was putting her four-year-old son Luke to bed when he exclaimed: "I'm exhausted!"

"Exhausted?" she said. "Who says that?"

"John Michael," replied Luke, who had been listening to a cassette by Christian singer John Michael Talbot. "You know the song that says, 'Be exhausted, O God, among the heavens.'"

After church one Sunday morning, a mother commented: "The choir was awful this morning." The father commented: "The sermon was too long."

Their seven-year-old daughter added: "You've got to admit it was a pretty good show for a dime."

—Joe Maher, Oxnard, California

The Family Circus

"We went to your house yesterday, but we couldn't find you."

Reprinted with permission of Bil Keane
from *Behold the Family Circus,* Thomas Nelson Publishers

I was driving my car when I noticed a young mother from our church walking with her four-year-old daughter. I slowed my car, rolled down the window, and spoke to them for a moment. After I drove away, the daughter looked up at her mother and asked, "Mommy, isn't that the man who hypnotized me when I was a baby?"

—Rev. John Riley, All Saints Episcopal Church, Jacksonville, Florida

Little John was bothered with a question that he had to ask his Sunday school teacher. "Miss Davis, are there any animals in heaven?"

"I'm not sure, Johnny," answered the teacher. "The Bible doesn't tell us of any animals in heaven."

"Oh, there's got to be animals in heaven," insisted Johnny.

"What makes you think so?" said the teacher.

"Well, every time there's a thunderstorm, my father says it's raining cats and dogs."

—Hal Wickliffe, Harrison, New York

F MC member Pastor Stan Holdeman of Garden Baptist Church, Indianapolis, Indiana, went to an informal church gathering, wearing shorts and a T-shirt. A little girl from a newly-churched family who had seen him only in his Sunday morning suits loudly proclaimed: "Hey, preacher, you sure look different with clothes on!"

B enjamin Leese, fifteen, who teaches Sunday school class for the third-graders at Trinity Lutheran Church, East Berlin, Pennsylvania, asked his students: "What is a prophet?"

One young boy quickly replied, "When someone makes a good investment."

O ur children's choir at Holy Faith Parish recently presented a dramatization of the Gospel parable of the Pharisee and the Publican. We fleshed it out with some humor and contemporary references. In the rehearsal (but fortunately, not in the actual presentation), one of the children read the Pharisee's prayer as follows: "O, God, I thank Thee that I am not like other people—a liar, cheat, nasty, dishonest, or worse—like that Republican over there."

—Rev. Jim Moss, Gainesville, Florida

F r. Harold Cost of Holy Family Church, Belle Prairie, Minnesota, recalls hearing the first confession of a second grader who had little to confess.

"Do you have any more?" the priest asked.

"Sure," the youngster replied, "but I'm saving some for next time."

—Joseph Young, **Saint Cloud** *(Minnesota)* **Visitor**

A third-grade religion class was reviewing the Ten Commandments. The teacher asked one youngster, "If mother told Johnny not to tease the dog and pull his tail and he did anyway, what commandment would he be breaking?"

The child responded, "I don't know the number of the commandment, but it says 'What God has joined together let no man pull apart.'"

—*Gertrude Golden, Euclid, Ohio*

The Family Circus

"Daddy, when are we goin' over to the confession stand?"

Reprinted with permission of Bil Keane

A sturdy eight-year-old boy went for his first confession to FMC member Fr. James Carroll, OMI, pastor of Parish of Blessed Eugene de Mazenod, in Burpengary, Australia. After a few words to put the boy at ease, Fr. Carroll asked: "Would you like to tell me your sins?"

"Sure," the boy answered. "Which ones do you want? The good ones or the bad ones?"

After telling her class the story of God's promise to give His people a land flowing with milk and honey, a Sunday school teacher asked her little ones: "What do you think a land flowing with milk and honey would be like?"

"I think it would be pretty sticky," Bobby replied.

—*Msgr. Arthur Tonne*

Our pastor, Bill Bader of St. Paul's Lutheran Church in Onalaska, Wisconsin, was delivering a children's sermon on the proper management of time. He asked the little ones seated on the floor around him, "Can you think of ways in which you waste time?" One three-year-old girl replied, "How about taking a bath?"

—*Dave Luetke*

The Family Circus

**"Does 'love thy neighbor' mean the people
on BOTH sides of our house?"**

Reprinted with permission of Bil Keane

Returning home from Sunday school, a little girl told how disappointed she was with the class reaction after the day's lesson.

"We were taught to go into all the world and make disciples of all nations," she said, "but we just sat."
—*Dick Van Dyke*

A small boy in Sunday school described how powerful God is: "God is more powerful than Batman, Superman, and the Lone Ranger put together."
—*Dick Van Dyke*

My six-year-old son and I were waiting at the curb to cross the street on the way home from Sunday school. The cars were speeding by. Dean looked up and asked, "Don't these people know that Presbyterians have the right of way?"
—*Elaine R. Wilcox*

When my son Jason was three years old, our church was meeting temporarily on Sunday mornings in a local school until we could move into a new building. To keep our folding chairs from being mistaken for those belonging to the school, we painted the word *JESUS* across the back of each of the chairs.

One day, as we were eating at a local restaurant, Jason proudly announced that he could spell *chair*. "How, Jason?" I asked. "J-E-S-U-S," he replied.
—*Candy Chester, Magnolia, Ohio*

My grandson, Benjamin, age three, was sitting with his mother, Jacqueline Lawrence, at St. Joseph's Church in Mechanicsburg, Pennsylvania. The priest, delivering an intense sermon on social problems, leaned toward the parishioners and said, "I'm serious." Benjamin looked up at the priest and replied, "I'm serious too."
—*Pastor Grace T. Lawrence, First Baptist Church, Lykens, Pennsylvania*

At a White House breakfast for religious leaders, President Bush told the story of a little boy who offered up this simple prayer: "God bless Mother and Daddy, my brother and sister; and God, do take care of Yourself because if anything happens to You, we're all sunk."

—ABA Banker's Weekly

The Family Circus

". . . and bless the hands that repaired this food."

Reprinted with permission of Bil Keane

A mother told her young son to go to bed and be sure to say his prayers and ask God to make him a good boy. The boy's father, passing by the bedroom, overheard his son praying: "And God make me a good boy if You can; and if You can't, don't worry about it, 'cause I'm having fun the way I am."

—*Msgr. Arthur Tonne*

WILL ROGERS NEVER MET A CHURCH HE DIDN'T LIKE

© 1996 Ed Sullivan

JN consulting editor Chaplain Cy Eberhart of Salem, Oregon, portrays the great American humorist Will Rogers in a touring performance called "Will Rogers, Live!" Packed with Rogers' whimsical observations on church/

Will Rogers Never Met a Church He Didn't Like   **51**

religion/preachers/politicians from the 1920s and 1930s. The performance received standing ovations when Eberhart performed at the Lyndon B. Johnson Presidential Library in Austin, Texas, and at the Herbert Hoover Presidential Library in West Branch, Iowa. The act also has the endorsement of the Will Rogers Memorial in Claremore, Oklahoma, where Eberhart did much of his research on Rogers. Eberhart shares the following reflections:

Will Rogers was a national treasure. One of the most beloved personalities in American history, Rogers had a powerful influence on the lives of Americans, lifting their spirits with laughter in the darkest of times.

Though he was raised a Methodist and later belonged to a Presbyterian church in Hollywood, California, Rogers had an expansive heart that embraced all faiths. Grady Nutt, the popular humorist who was also a Baptist pastor, once said of Rogers, "He (Jesus) makes the most sense to me, the most profound impact on me, when I envision him as Will Rogers in sandals."

This gentle and merry-hearted cowboy of Native American descent could never say no to anyone in need, and gave his time and money to countless charities. He was the very model of a cheerful giver.

An independent, Rogers never aligned himself with any political party. He enjoyed teasing both parties, but his remarks always were without rancor. In 1928, *Life* magazine, which started out as a humor magazine, nominated him as the presidential candidate for the "Anti-Bunk Party."

It was Rogers who said, "I never met a man I didn't like." He also never met a church or a synagogue he didn't like. He was often invited to speak in churches, and he invariably left the congregations howling with laughter, and strengthened in their faith.

When he was killed in an airplane crash in Alaska, the national mourning was on a scale that only the most beloved of American presidents have received when they died.

Here is some of Rogers' wit and wisdom, which tickled the funny bones of so many congregations and organizations and which have stood the test of time:

"We are getting to be a nation that can't read anymore. That's why the Bible is not read more than it is. If some preacher was just smart enough to put the Bible into a crossword puzzle, the entire United States would know it by heart."

"I attended the opening ceremonies at the Olympics in Los Angeles, and the only test of endurance was a 10,000-meter prayer. A man with a short prayer could get a booking for life just at these national events."

"I think we'd get a whole lot more accomplished in our meetings if you all weren't so negative."

© 1996 Dik LaPine

"We in California maintain more freak religions and cults than all the rest of the world combined. Just start anything out here and if it's cuckoo enough, you will get followers."

"If some of these folks would spend their time following His example instead of trying to figure out His mode of arrival and departure, they would come nearer getting confidence in their church."

ON CONTEMPORARY PREACHERS

"Now P. T. Barnum invented the tent, but Billy Sunday filled it. He's the only man in ecclesiastical or biblical history that ever had to train physically for a sermon. I discovered Billy Sunday and William Jennings Bryan preaching in a tent in the wilds of this village. Now you can always attract a crowd to a tent, for they figure it might be a circus. Their acts were similar; either one of them could take a dictionary and sink an enemy with words at 40 paces."

"Sister (Aimee) McPherson (Semple) sent an advisory out to invite me as her special guest to her new musical play based on the Bible— words by Moses, music by McPherson. Now she has gone and got married on me. Hollywood may not keep you young, but it sure keeps you marrying."

"I closed one night with the Follies and opened the next night in a church in Elmira, New York. It was Henry Ward Beecher's church. The only ones I had any trouble with were the regular church members who were occupying their regular pews. They just naturally went to sleep out of force of habit. I couldn't keep them awake. The only way I got them out of there was to say 'Amen' at the finish. Now in making this tremendous leap from the Follies to the pulpit, I would like to state that I did not have to change one word of my act."

ON POLITICIANS AND PREACHERS

"Politics hits a country like a pestilence. There is no telling where it will hit. This year, the churches are hit by it harder than usual. It has been the text of more sermons than the Lord's Supper. A minister can't pray without asking divine assistance in the election of his man. Before he says 'Amen,' he takes a poll vote. Half the contributions go into the campaign fund."

"A preacher just can't save anybody nowadays. He is too busy saving the nation. He can't monkey with individual salvation. In the old days, those fellows read their Bibles. Now they read the Congressional Record.

"If Congress met on Sundays, why there wouldn't be any services anywhere; all the ministers would have their eyes on Congress."

"Today being Sunday, even in a political convention, I just got an idea I would see just how religious all these politicians really are. So I grab a cab and rush from one church to the other all over town, and not a single candidate, or delegate, or even delegates, was among the worshipers.

"Still, this fall, in the campaign, you will hear them get up and shout, 'Our religion is the bulwark of our great and glorious country; we must continue to be God-fearing people; our church is our salvation.' Well, our churches are our salvation, but some of those babies won't be among those rescued."

"During a filibuster, one Senator threatened to read the entire Bible into the record, and I guess he would have if anyone in the Senate had a Bible."

"Elections are a good deal like marriages—there's no accounting for anyone's taste. Every time we see a bridegroom we wonder why she ever picked him, and it's the same with public officials."

"Remember this about politicians—all politicians are smarter than the people who elected them."

"The minute a thing is long and complicated, it confuses. Whoever wrote the Ten Commandments made 'em short. They may not always be kept, but they can be understood. They are the same for all men. Some industry can't come in and say, 'Ours is a special and unique business. You can't judge it by the others.'

Will Rogers Never Met a Church He Didn't Like **55**

"Moses just went up on the mountain with some instructions from the Lord, and He just wrote 'em out, and they applied to the steel men, the oil men, the bankers, the farmers, and even the United States Chamber of Commerce. And he said, 'Here they are, brother; you take 'em and live by 'em, or else.'"

"I don't care what your religion is, what your belief is; individuals and political parties, especially, can learn much from the pope of the Catholic Church. When you read what the pope says, you don't have to start wondering, or asking your neighbor what he meant; he says what he meant."

"You hear or read sermons nowadays and the biggest part of it is taken up knocking or trying to prove the falseness of some other denomination. Now just suppose, for a change, they preached to you about the Lord and not about the other fellow's church, for every man's religion is good. Hunt out and talk about the good that is in the other fellow's church, not the bad, and you will do away with all this religious hatred you hear so much of nowadays. . . . If they are going to argue religion in the church, instead of teaching it, no wonder you can see more people at a circus than at a church."

SAY NOTHING OFTEN

"I heard you were here, Pastor, but I didn't want to cancel our counseling session."

© 1996 Steve Phelps

Two quick ways to disaster: 1) Take nobody's advice. 2) Take everybody's advice.

—*Ralph Cansler, Cohutta, Georgia*

FMC member Rev. John J. Kelley, OMI, Catholic chaplain at the Deuel Vocational Institution in Tracy, California, collected these one-liners on the subject of giving advice:

" **B**e yourself" is about the worst advice you can give to some people."

"Advice is that which the wise don't need, and the fool won't take."

"The trouble with giving advice is that people want to repay you."

"It's extremely difficult to take advice from some people when they need it more than you do."

"The best advice: Say nothing often."

In the early part of this century, the London Times *asked several eminent authors to write articles on the theme, "What's Wrong with the World?" Christian humorist G. K. Chesterton wrote this brief reply:*

Dear Sirs:
I am.
Sincerely yours,
G. K. Chesterton

A gossip is one who talks to you about other people.

A bore is one who talks to you about himself.

A brilliant conversationalist is one who talks to you about yourself.

—*Dr. William King,* **Apple Seeds**

JN contributing cartoonist Steve Phelps of Sapulpa, Oklahoma, writes:

"**D**id you hear the one about the little old lady from church? She doesn't repeat gossip—so you'd better listen the first time!"

Live so that you wouldn't be ashamed to sell the family parrot to the town gossip.

—*Will Rogers*

THE DOG AS COUNSELOR

Can dogs possess insight humans lack? FMC member Msgr. Lonnie C. Reyes of St. Julia Catholic Church, Austin, Texas, whose miniature poodle Mr. Deauveaureaux lives with him in the rectory, seems to think so. He once counseled a mother and her fourteen-year-old daughter to get a dog to help resolve an interminable and hostile impasse between them over the daughter's dating habits.

"Get a dog and the dog will tell you the type of person the boy is," Fr. Reyes advised. "If he is inattentive and bothered by the dog, eventually he will be inattentive and bothered by you. If the dog barks at him and does not want to be near him, beware of the guy."

Dogs have so many friends because they wag their tails, not their tongues.

—*Anonymous*

Fr. Reyes notes that St. Bernard once wrote: "Who loves me loves my dog."

He tells this story about the time God gave St. Peter a vacation from his duty at the Pearly Gates, and assigned two dogs at the gate:

"When a person approached Heaven's gate and the dogs trembled with fear or barked and growled, that person was not allowed to enter. But if the dogs wagged their tails and jumped with joy, that person was welcomed into the eternal bliss of Heaven.

"**A**s I approached the pearly gates and saw St. Peter frowning there my heart sank with a heavy weight so grave was his face and stern his stare. But Schroder wagged his tail in greeting and Tashi jumped into my arms. I was glad to see them at this meeting and so forgot all my alarm.

"St. Peter's list proved me a sinner, but he tore it up and then decreed: 'Won't use this; you're a winner. Your friends are all the proof I need.'"

—*FMC member Jim Young, Gainesville, Florida*

A young preacher had been called to a small rural church and appeared for his first sermon on Sunday morning. To his dismay he found that one of the parishioners had brought his dog to the service. He spoke politely to the dog's owner and asked if he would kindly remove the animal. The man obligingly took the dog out, then returned to his seat.

After the service, the church deacons rebuked the new preacher for insulting one of their staunch members. They pointed out that the dog made no trouble; he had been accompanying his master to church for years.

That afternoon the young preacher called at the home of the dog's owner and apologized.

"Don't worry a bit about it, Reverend," the man replied, "It all worked out. I wouldn't have had my dog hear that sermon for anything in the world."

—*Sherwood Eliot Wirt,* **The Book of Joy**

A Young Pastor's First Baptismal Service

A dunk-tank baptismal pool would prove to be a tough-sell for church supply salesman Bob Stevens.

© 1996 Bill Frauhiger

The country church was located so far out in the woods that there was no indoor plumbing. However, since baptism was an important part of the church's life, the congregation improvised by building a baptistry under the pulpit. When it came time to baptize, they moved the pulpit aside, opened the trap door, filled the baptistry with water hauled by a large tank truck, dropped some wooden stairs down into it, and strung up some curtains.

The thick curtains were carefully hung on wires. One curtain served as a backdrop to the baptistry and was pulled around in a circular position. The curtains were also arranged so they provided a men's dressing room on one side of the baptistry and a women's dressing room on the other side.

The young pastor of this country church was to baptize his first two candidates—an elderly man and a heavy-set lady. On the evening of the baptismal service, one deacon waited in the baptistry with the pastor, and another deacon carefully helped the elderly gentleman down the stairs. After he was baptized, the deacon in the baptistry helped him up the stairs and followed him back behind the curtains to the dressing room. But no one thought to help the young pastor with the baptism of the heavy-set lady.

Excited, the woman stepped into the baptistry on the first step. The wooden steps, slick from standing under water so long, proved to be her downfall. Her feet slipped, and she promptly sat down on the top step. Then, one by one, she bounced down into the baptistry in the sitting position.

They claim you could hear her scream a mile away. Screaming and bouncing down the stairs, she reached up to grab the only object available—the curtains! So, down into the baptistry with the screaming lady came the men's dressing room and the women's dressing room!

There, visible to the eyes of the whole congregation was the elderly gentleman in the process of getting dressed. He had already donned his longhandled underwear and was in the process of pulling up his trousers. He dropped his trousers to the floor and stood paralyzed, staring at the surprised congregation. Then, he picked up a nearby chair and held it in front of him.

"Do something quick!" one of the deacons shouted. So, a thoughtful deacon ran to the back and turned off all the lights, thinking that the man would take the hint to get dressed in the darkness.

Five minutes later when the lights were turned back on, the man was still standing there in his longhandled underwear, protecting himself with the chair. The lady, still gurgling and bubbling in the water was fighting the curtains. The young pastor, in shock, was standing in the corner of the baptistry with his arms folded and his eyes staring straight ahead!

A small country church was having a "baptizing" in a river on a cold January day. A revival meeting had just concluded. The preacher asked one baptismal candidate, "Is the water cold?"

"Naw!" he replied.

One of the deacons shouted: "Dip him agin' preacher, he's still lyin'!"

—*This chapter's excerpts taken from* **The Treasury of Clean Church Jokes** *by Tal D. Bonham (Nashville: Broadman & Holman Publishers, © 1986). Reprinted with permission. Available from the Fellowship of Merry Christians catalog or your local bookstore.*

CHAPTER
10

WORD
GAMES

The Final Fixing of the Foolish Fugitive—a Parable

Rev. W. O. Taylor, 91, was the oldest man attending the Southern Baptist Convention a few years ago. At the annual free breakfast for retirees, Brother Taylor rose and recited his own alliterative version of the parable of the prodigal son, which he entitled "The Final Fixing of the Foolish Fugitive":

"Feeling footloose, fancy-free and frisky, this feather-brained fellow finagled his fond father into forking over his fortune. Forthwith, he fled for foreign fields and frittered his farthings feasting fabulously with fair-weather friends. Finally, facing famine, and fleeced by his fellows in folly, he found himself a feed flinger in a filthy farmlot. He fain would have filled his frame with foraged food from the fodder fragments.

"'Fooey! My father's flunkies fare far fancier,' the frazzled fugitive fumed feverishly, frankly facing fact.

"Frustrated from failure and filled with forebodings, he fled for his family.

"Falling at his father's feet, he floundered forlornly. 'Father, I have flunked and fruitlessly forfeited further family favors . . .'

"But the faithful father, forestalling further flinching, frantically flagged his flunkies to fetch forth the finest fatling and fix a feast.

"But the fugitive's fault-finding frater, faithfully farming his father's fields for free, frowned at this fickle forgiveness of former falderal. His fury flashed, but fussing was futile.

"His foresighted father figured, 'Such filial fidelity is fine, but what forbids fervent festivities? The fugitive is found! Unfurl the flags! With fanfare flaring, let fun, frolic and frivolity flow freely, former failures forgotten and folly forsaken. Forgiveness forms a firm foundation for future fortitude.'"

Q: What do you call the people who regularly evacuate the rear pew at the sound of the first note of the recessional hymn and well before the priest exits?
A: The faithful departed.
> —*Fr. Raymond G. Heisel, Church of the Epiphany/Church of St. Rose Sodus, New York*

Q: How many prophets does it take to screw in a light bulb?
A: Two. One to screw in the light bulb and one to curse him for living in darkness.
> —*Brian Irving, the Raleigh, North Carolina, LIMEX Group*

Q: What did the Buddhist monk say to the hot dog vendor at the ballpark?
A: Make me one with everything.
> —*George Goldtrap, Madison, Tennessee*

Q: What do you get when you play New Age music backward?
A: New Age music.

A Soapy Prayer

Almighty and eternal Father, help us to no longer be *The Young and the Restless*. Help us to build a *Dynasty*. Let us remain close to You, walking not in *Ryan's Hope*, but in Christian hope, for our destination is heaven and not *Dallas*. May the parents of Your community always say to You: "Bless and protect *All My Children*." Truly these are *The Days of Our Lives*. And so, *As the World Turns*, and some of us have to visit *The Doctors* and *General Hospital*, may we ever keep You, dear

Lord, as our *Guiding Light*. Then, we will not be concerned with a foolish *Search for Tomorrow,* waiting on *The Edge of Night;* for together, Lord, we can forget about *Knot's Landing* and build *Another World*. Amen.

—*Anonymous*

The Pit

A man fell into a pit and couldn't get himself out.

A *subjective* person came along and said, "I feel for you down there."

An *objective* person walked by and said, "It's logical that someone would fall down there."

A *Pharisee* said, "Only bad people fall into pits."

A *mathematician* calculated how he fell into the pit.

A *news reporter* wanted the exclusive story on the pit.

An *IRS agent* asked if he was paying taxes on the pit.

A *self-pitying* person said, "You haven't seen anything until you've seen my pit!"

A *fire-and-brimstone preacher* said, "You deserve your pit."

A *Christian Scientist* observed, "The pit is just in your mind."

A *psychologist* noted, "Your mother and father are to blame for your being in that pit."

A *self-esteem therapist* said, "Believe in yourself and you can get out of that pit."

An *optimist* said, "Things could be worse."

A *pessimist* claimed, "Things *will* get worse."

Jesus, seeing the man, took him by the hand and lifted him out of the pit.

—*Church bulletin in Australia*

FMC member William G. Campbell of St. Saviour's Anglican Church, Vermilion, Alberta, calls hymn #521 in the Book of Common Praise *of the Anglican Church of Canada "the dry cleaners hymn":*

"O for a faith that will not shrink
Though pressed by many a foe."

An optimist is a man who puts on his shoes when, during a sermon, the preacher says, "Finally."
—*Very Rev. Nathan D. Baxter, Dean, Washington Cathedral*

In the *Spokane* (Washington) *Spokesman* newspaper, columnist Paul Turner related this story from a friend: "While visiting my wife's parents in Maryland, we stopped on the Delaware shore at a small doughnut shop called Dough and Cin. Just think, if the place ever went out of business, they could call it Dough and Cin No More."

When Eugene Field was a newspaper reporter in Chicago, he wrote in his column: "Half the aldermen in the city are crooks." The mayor demanded a retraction, so the next day Field wrote: "Half the alderman in the city are not crooks."

The Lawyer's Hymn: "Just as I am, Without One Plea."
—*Andy Fisher, Denville, New Jersey*

Ecumenism: Getting to know the opposite sects.
—*Ron Birk, San Marcos, Texas*

Why is it that "fat chance" and "slim chance" mean the same thing?
—*Eugene L. Smith, Booneville, Arkansas*

An egotist is someone who is always me-deep in conversation.
—*George Goldtrap*

Politically Correct Lord's Prayer

Our universal chairperson in outer space, your identity enjoys the highest rating on a prioritized selectivity scale. May your sphere of influence take on reality parameters; may your mindset be implemented on this planet as in outer space.

Allot to us at this point in time and on a per diem basis, a sufficient and balanced dietary food intake, and rationalize a disclaimer against our negative feedback as we rationalize the negative feedback of others.

And deprogram our negative potentialities, but desensitize the impact of the counterproductive force. For yours is the dominant sphere of influence, the ultimate capability and the highest qualitative analysis rating, at this point in time and extending beyond a limited time-frame. End of message.

SIGNS AND WONDERS

Seen on a church sign:

"If evolution is true, why do mothers still have only two hands?"
—*Rev. Tim Davis, Westmount Park Church, Toronto, Canada*

In a sermon at First United Methodist Church, the Reverend P. Thomas Wachterhauser observed: "Have you noticed the problem created for ministers by the large bulletin boards out in front of a church? The sermon title is placed just above the name of the preacher of the day. A year ago, the sign read: "Who killed Jesus? Dr. Alfred T. Bamsey." Not long ago, the sign read: "Nothing to Wear. Rev. Marsha M. Woolley." This morning, the sign reads: "The Perfect Christian. Rev. P. Thomas Wachterhauser."
—*Winslow Fox, M.D., Ann Arbor, Michigan*

A popular speaker on humor and healing, Sister Mary Christelle Macaluso, RSM, aka "The Fun Nun," who lives in Omaha, Nebraska, says she once drove by a church sign that read: "Jesus Saves." Directly across the street was a grocery store sign: "We save you more!"

Sign in Internal Revenue Service office:

In God we trust; everyone else we audit.

On an outdoor sign at Northway Christian Church (Disciples of Christ) in Dallas, Texas:

Premarital Workshop
8 hours May 17 & 18
Grief Recovery
Starts Tuesday May 21

JN member Marius Risley of Buffalo, New York, saw this sign in an Episcopal church parking lot:

Clergy Space
You park
You preach

St. More or Less

St. James the Less Catholic Church in Highland, Indiana, received hundreds of phone calls after the church put up this new outdoor sign:

St. James
the Less
Catholic
Church

Father Francis Lazar said he "got calls from Catholics wanting to know if the church was offering an easier way to practice their faith and if we still believe in everything the Catholic Church teaches. Of course, we do."

—*Andy Fisher,* **JN** *consulting editor and senior writer*
for NBC's **Today Show**

A church bulletin announced the coffee hour:

Thirst after Righteousness.

—*Dick Friedline, First Christian Church, Ventura, California*

A BUMPER CROP

"**D**efining ourselves is a characteristic of our culture," write FMC members Jeanne and Owen Welles of Florence, Oregon. "This is seen by the way we use and/or personalize T-shirts, baseball caps, haircuts, and, especially, bumper stickers.

"It occurred to us to ask what the people in the Old and New Testaments would have put on their bumper stickers or T-shirts. Consider the possibilities":

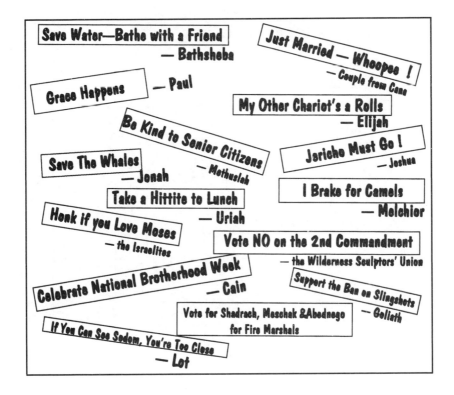

Message on an outdoor church sign:

If you have insomnia, don't count sheep. Talk to the Shepherd.

During an August heat wave, FMC member Mrs. Robert LaBerge of Lake Orion, Michigan, saw this message on an outdoor church sign: And you think it's hot here?

BULLETIN BLOOPERS THAT GNASH THE TEETH

© 1996 Harley L. Schwadron

Church bulletin and newsletter editors are not alone in being bedeviled by typos and misprints. Max Hall, of Cambridge, Massachusetts, a former Associated Press Washington correspondent, has zealously collected misprints in publications for much of his 86 years. Hall is the author of a book called *An Embarrassment of Misprints* (Golden, Colorado: Fulcrum Publishing, © 1995), a collection of comical typos through the centuries.

In a *Harvard Magazine* article, Hall noted that a 1961 international edition of *The New York Times* referred to the then-Archbishop of Canterbury as "the red-nosed Archbishop"—rather than red-robed. And an *Atlanta Constitution* editor once scribbled this headline late one night: "Land Grants in Hall" (meaning Hall County). It came out in the paper as "Loud Grunts in Hell."

Misprints in Bibles have also been common, observed Hall. An unidentified 16th-century monk once attributed typographical errors and misprints to "the doings of the devil." Hall passed on to the editor of *JN* a passage from *Curiosities of Literature, Volume 1* (1823) by Isaac D'Israeli, the father of British Prime Minister Benjamin Disraeli (the names are spelled differently): "In the year 1561 was printed a work entitled *The Anatomy of the Mass*. It is a thin octavo of 172 pages, and it is accompanied by an Errata of 15 pages. (Editor's note: Errata are a list of errors with their corrections, inserted on a separate page or pages of published work.)

"The editor, a pious Monk . . . supposes that the Devil, to ruin the fruit of this work . . . obliged the printers to commit such numerous blunders never yet equaled in so small a work."

D'Israeli then observed that one dreadful Bible misprint in 1631 omitted the word *not* from Exodus 20:14, so that it said, "Thou shalt commit adultery." D'Israeli also noted that The Vinegar Bible (1717) was so named because the heading over Luke 20, the Parable of the Vineyard, was misprinted as "The Parable of the Vinegar."

As time marched on, an apprentice in a print shop came to be known as a "printer's devil."

The Devil's Pi

In 1941, Eli Cantor, who was the owner of a typesetting firm in the days of linotype and at one time was board chairman of Printing Industries of America, authored a satirical little book called *The Devil's Pi* ("Pi" is a printer's term for type that is spilled or mixed.)

Cantor fleshed out the "strange legend" of the devil and printshops. "Satan and his host were bored in hell," Cantor wrote, "but after the invention of movable type by the German printer Gutenberg (1400–68 A.D.), Satan decided to keep his legions of demons entertained by inventing a new mischief.

He sent his devils and demons out to "cause such consternation among printers and all associated with them as will make them wish they had never been born!"

Satan divided up his legion of demons into separate armies. One army was ordered to "mix up the letters, confuse spaces, throw away type, drop wrong fonts into cases, make every typecase look as if an earthquake hit it."

Another army of demons was ordered "to specialize in faulty punctuation, mix up periods, commas, apostrophes, semi-colons, substituting one for another, causing them to be left out, or placed where they do not belong."

Still another army of demons was commanded to "transpose letters and words, causing wrong letters to be used."

"Since that fearful day when those pestilent armies swarmed out of hell to invade the printshops of the world," Cantor observed, "no printer or typesetter or user of printing has had a moment of peace."

Publications and printers hired proofreaders to catch and correct the errors made by demons. But Satan held them in contempt. "If you mean those feeble creatures who try to stand against our attacks," Satan told one of his demons, "I can assure you that for every error they correct they let hundreds pass."

Is there a better explanation for bloopers and misprints? We think not. But the appropriate Christian response to the devil's mischief in printshops is not anger, but laughter. As St. Francis of Assisi, Martin Luther, and many others have observed, the devil can't stand the sound of laughter.

Just for laughs, here are some of our favorite bloopers, mostly from church bulletins and newsletters, from the first ten years of *The Joyful Noiseletter*:

From a Baptist church bulletin:

"There is joy in the presence of the angles over one singer who repents."

—The Baptist Record, *Jackson, Mississippi*

From The Word *newsletter of the Fellowship of Christian Ministers, Indianapolis, Indiana:*

"**C**huck McNeeley challenged those who attended this year's retreat with four messages about Holiness . . . available on audiotape for $5.50 each.

    1. Becoming the Holy Man.

    2. Delivering the Holy Massage."

From Australia come these church bulletin bloopers, passed on by FMC member Dr. Geoff Pankhurst, pastor of the Uniting Church in Orange, Australia:

"**T**hursday night—Potluck Supper. Prayer and medication to follow."

"**F**or those of you who have children and don't know it, we have a nursery downstairs."

After an earthquake struck the Philippines, a Uniting Church Mission publication reprinted photos of the earthquake damage with this caption: "Most of the photos included here were taken one week after the largest eruption by Leonie Purcival, A Uniting Church member."

FMC member Fr. Joseph L. Stahura, pastor of St. Mark the Evangelist Church, Greencastle, Pennsylvania, says his secretary provided the company that produces his church bulletin with information about a meeting of a Catholic women's organization named after Mother Seton at St. Ignatius Parish. Couples celebrating their 25th and 50th wedding anniversaries were to be honored. Fr. Stahura's secretary was dismayed when the announcement was printed as follows:

"**S**ATAN DISTRICT 25th–50th Anniversary Celebration, September 29, 1996, at St. Ignatious Parish, Buchanan Valley. Mass at 2 P.M. followed by reception."

Early warning signs of pastoral burnout.

© 1996 Jonny Hawkins

"**A**ll the youth choirs of Our Redeemer have been disbanded for the summer with the thanks of the entire church."

From the Holy Week bulletin of St. John's Anglican Church, Edmonton, Alberta:

"**M**aundy Thursday, April 8, 7 P.M. We will re-enact the Last Supper and journey to the Garden of Gethsemane. We will strip the altar and sanctuary of all color and symbol. Together, we will leave the church bare and in silence."

From Lenten bulletin of Zion Lutheran Church, Garretson, South Dakota:

"**7**:30 LENTEN SERVICE. The final Lenten Service theme is: 'Why Doesn't God Do Something?' with Pastor Meidinger."

In the bulletin of the Westchester (Illinois) Community United Church of Christ:

"**A**nd we give you thanks, O God, for people of many cultures and nations; for the young and old and muddle-aged."

FMC member Rev. Grace T. Lawrence, pastor of the First Baptist Church of Lykens, Pennsylvania, writes that the church's "Good News Letter" carried the following report on the prayer group meeting:

"**O**n March 16th, the prayer group met at the home of Margaret Ressler, who is no longer able to attend church. What a blessing!"

From the newsletter of St. Matthews Lutheran Church, St. Paul, Minnesota:

"**A**DULT FORUM. Beginning November 5, Pastor Hodges will lead a six-part series on the book of Genesis. Were Adam and Eve really naked in the Garden? Come and see for yourself."
—*Palmer Ruschke, St. Paul, Minnesota*

Pastor Wesley Macy, at Estes Brook Evangelical Free Church in Foley, Minnesota, sent this blooper—a bulletin insert with the words to the song "O Worship the King," which read:

"**O** Worship the King, all glorious above, and gratefully sin . . . ."

The Midway Presbyterian Church of Decatur, Georgia, has a time in the order of worship for "Silent Meditation." One Sunday it came out in the church bulletin as "Silent Medication."
—*Rev. Woody McKay*

From the First Methodist Church, Athens, Ohio:

"**R**emember how Jesus compared the kingdom to a treasurer hidden in a field?"

From the yearbook of Trinity Lutheran Church, Jeffers, Minnesota:

"The (correspondence) committee will assist with the mailing of the newsletter and stapling of the Annual Report to congregational members."

Blooper in the Call to Worship in the bulletin of First Presbyterian Church, Springfield, Tennessee:

PASTOR: "Happy are those who find joy in obeying the Law of the Lord . . ."
PEOPLE: "We shall sin with joyfulness to the Lord our God!"

In the church newsletter, our chairman of Christian education expressed concern about the Sunday school students who were arriving late every morning as follows:

"When the opening is delayed due to stranglers, it cuts into the time that the teachers have to spend with your children sharing God's word."

—Rev. Dann J. Ettner, Atwater, California

From the bulletin of Muhlenberg Lutheran Church, Harrisonburg, Virginia:

"The annual fund-raising event for Luther Crest Auxiliary is being held May 6 from 1 to 5 P.M. Hot dogs and drinks will be available for purchase as well as a baked goof you wish to donate to the baked goods table."

—Dr. Richard Schiemann, Harrisonburg, Virginia

One Mother's Day, we used a variation of the hymn "Faith of Our Fathers," titled "Faith of Our Mothers," but it appeared as "Faith of Our Moths."

—Rev. April L. Michaelsen, Sons of Zebedee Lutheran Church, Saltsburg, Pennsylvania

MADCAP MISPRINTS FROM HERE AND THERE

Computer misprint in the Lenten calendar of St. Lawrence the Martyr Church, Chester, New Jersey:

"April 4
Palm Sunday
Palms symbolize victory over death by Jesus who was unable to attend church. Resurrection. Give a palm branch to someone who was unable to attend church."

When prophets debate.

© 1996 Dik LaPine

Evangelist Billy Graham, advising a young virgin in high school to remain celibate in his syndicated column in The Arizona Republic

"The Bible is clear: 'Flee from sexual immortality.' "
—*Gina Bridgeman, Scottsdale, Arizona*

Typo in a September 3 circular letter to priests in Philadelphia from Rev. Hans A. L. Brouwers, archdiocesan director, concerning preparations for World Mission Sunday, October 24:

"You will soon receive, as part of the September archdiocesan Priest's Monthly Mailing, a Liturgy Guide, and a Massage of His Holiness Pope John Paul II for World Mission Sunday."

Friends of ours with whom we served as missionaries in Nepal wrote to us the following story:

As we were purchasing supplies from a yet unmet vendor, we identified our organization over the phone as Mennonite Disaster Service. The goods arrived at the job site, and the billing was addressed to Many-a-Night Disaster Service.

—*Rev. Thomas L. Harrington, Blairsville, Georgia*

"Harpeth Hills Church of Christ, 1949 Old Hickory Blvd., Nashville, Tennessee, will present a series of community classes on various subjects throughout this month and into March. The classes offered include: 'How to Lose 100 Pounds, from 7–9 P.M. Monday.'"

—*George Goldtrap, Madison, Tennessee*

While vacationing in Ocean City, New Jersey, FMC member Pastor Grace T. Lawrence of First Baptist Church, Lykens, Pennsylvania, spotted this blooper in the local newspaper:

"Lloyd John Ogilvie, dynamic world-famous pastor and chaplain of the U.S. Senate, will appear at the Ocean City Tabernacle September 17. His duties include counseling and spiritual care for the Senators, their families, and their staffs—a combined consistency of over 6,000."

Reviewing *New York Times* reporter Tad Szulc's new book, *Pope John Paul II: The Biography*, columnist George Weigel noted that Szulc "had Cardinal Eugene Tisserant presiding over a conclave that took place six years after Tisserant's death."

FMC member Pastor David P. Buuck of Bethlehem Lutheran Church, Minnetonka, Minnesota, reports that his church has been receiving catalogs addressed to "Bethlehem L. Chu." One computerized letter declared: "We're waiting to hear from *you*, Bethlehem L. Chu!" Another computerized letter offered: "Liberal credit plan to fit the Chu family budget!"

> *Valerie Wells, religion and family news reporter for the Decatur, Illinois,* Herald & Review, *received the following announcement:*

"Please make this announcement for Women's Aglow in Decatur. On July 17, _____ will share with the women how God set her free from alcoholism and gave her back her husband after an almost fatal death."

FUNNY FLUBS FROM STUDENT ESSAYS AND EXAMS

Richard "The Abbot of Absurdity" Lederer, author of Anguished English, More Anguished English, *and* Get Thee to a Punnery, *passed on the following bloopers from essays and exams written by Sunday school students:*

"Esau was a man who wrote fables and sold his copyright for a mess of potash."

"The brother of Jacob was called Seesaw."

"Samson pulled down the pillows of the temple."

"The Israelites made a golden calf because they didn't have enough gold to make a cow."

"Joshua led the Hebrews in their victory in the battle of Geritol."

"**S**olomon had 200 wives and 700 cucumbers."

"**T**he people who followed the Lord were called the 12 opossums."

"**A** republican is a sinner mentioned in the Bible."

"**J**oan of Arc was burnt to a steak."

"**M**artin Luther was on a Diet of Worms."

"**S**hakespeare wrote his plays in Islamic pentameter."

"Thank you, sir. I ain't never gonna forget today."

© 1995 Harley L. Schwadron

© 1996 Goddard Sherman

SLIP OF THE LIP

JN *consulting editor Joe Garagiola passed on this blooper by Fr. Eric Tellez, associate pastor at St. Maria Goretti Catholic Church in Scottsdale, Arizona:*

During his homily, Fr. Tellez was discussing the folly of making the pursuit of happiness more important than God in one's life.

"When we pursue happiness as an end in itself, we are committing adultery . . . I mean idolatry," Fr. Tellez said.

There was a deafening silence, and then the entire congregation exploded with laughter.

Reading from Mark 1:9 one recent morning, FMC member Rev. Steven A. Becker, pastor of Theresa Presbyterian Church, Theresa, New York, transposed a couple of words and it came out: "At that time Jesus came from Nazareth in Galilee and was baptized by Jordan in the John."

In a slip of the tongue during his Sunday sermon, Rev. Mel Merwald, pastor of St. Margaret Mary Church, Omaha, Nebraska, referred to a reading from Deuteronomy as a reading from "debauchery."

—*Lilli Vorse, Council Bluffs, Iowa*

Eat Your Edible Bulletin and Reduce Church Litter

I substitute for weekend liturgies in many Catholic churches, and almost everywhere I go, I see untidy parishioners leaving a trail of debris. First of all, the untidy parishioner takes a church bulletin before Mass and reads it before and during the Mass, sometimes during the homily. He never takes it with him or replaces it. Hence, someone must follow him to clean up his litter. If he uses the missalette or hymnal, they, too, are left for someone else to pick up.

I've been thinking about this problem for some time and may be on the verge of a revolutionary solution. I'm testing an edible bulletin.

One flavor would not satisfy everyone. Perhaps a choice of vanilla, strawberry, or chocolate would be acceptable to most untidy parishioners. In fact, we may be stumbling upon another community-builder here. People might begin to swap their copy with those around them, perhaps at the sign of peace. The final dismissal rite might add "to love and serve the Lord and don't forget to eat your bulletin."

At any rate, the pews would be tidy after Masses, if I can come up with a solution for the disposal of bulletin crumbs.

—*FMC member Fr. Paul Mueller, St. Thomas More University Parish, Bowling Green, Ohio*

Note: What's a church to do when the parishioners give up eating their edible bulletins for Lent?

© 1996 Steve Phelps

EASTER LAUGHS

B.C.   By Johnny Hart

© 1995 Creators Syndicate, Inc.
Reprinted with permission of Johnny Hart & Creators Syndicate, Inc.

Fr. Richard Carton, associate pastor of St. Catherine of Siena Church, Mountain Lakes, New Jersey, was speaking to a group of second graders about the resurrection when one student asked, "What did Jesus say right after He came out of the grave?"

It was a question of great theological importance, but Fr. Carton had to explain, in words suitable to his young audience, that the Gospels do not tell us just what He said.

The hand of one little girl shot up. "I know what He said, Father," she insisted.

"And what was that?" asked Fr. Carton.

"Tah-dah!" the girl exclaimed.

—*Andy Fisher, Denville, New Jersey*

It was Easter Saturday, and FMC member Joanne Hinch of Woodland Hills, California, was sitting at the kitchen table coloring Easter eggs with her son, Dan, 3, and her daughter, Debby, 2. She told her children about the true meaning of Easter, and taught them the traditional Easter morning greeting, "He is risen!" and the reply, "He is risen, indeed!"

The children planned to surprise their father, a Presbyterian minister, with this greeting on Easter Sunday morning by saying "He is risen!" as soon as he awoke. The next morning, bright and early, little Dan heard his father arising in the bedroom, and raced down the hallway shouting, "Daddy, God's back!"

The Flock

"We celebrate the Passover at our church. At the first hint of controversy, we close our eyes and hope it will pass over."

© 1996 Larry White

The family of FMC member Rev. Ronald J. Volek of Guardian Angels Church, Copley, Ohio, gathered at his home for Easter Sunday dinner. Volek's three-year-old granddaughter, Samantha, cracked an Easter egg, removed the yolk, and holding it in her hand, asked: "And this is what part?"

"That is what would become a chick when the hen sits on the egg," her grandmother replied.

Samantha's older brother, Daniel, 6, added: "But first the rooster has to cock-a-doodle-doo."

The week before Easter is known as Holy Week because of its special significance to Christians. During this past Holy Week, a first-grade teacher at the local Lutheran school took great pains to explain all the events in Jesus' life that led up to the first Easter. She told them about Palm Sunday, and Maundy Thursday, and Good Friday, and finally Easter.

When she thought she had explained everything there was to know about that special week, the teacher asked if the students had any questions. One curious little boy raised his hand and asked, "What happens if you don't want to be holy all week?"
    —*Daniel Hintz, Grand Isle, Nebraska*

A pastor observed: "We certainly believe in the resurrection at our church. If you doubt it, just visit our offices sometime and watch our staff come back to life at quitting time."
    —*Tal Bonham*

The only thing some folks give up for Lent are their New Year's resolutions.
    —*Rev. Felix A. Lorenz Jr., Northville, Michigan*

You have to believe in happiness
Or happiness never comes . . .
Oh, that's the reason a bird can sing—
On his darkest day he believes in spring.
    —*Catherine Hall, Pittsburgh, Pennsylvania*

A preacher in Chilhowie, Virginia, was visiting a perennial church no-show in his home. "All right," the man finally said. "I'll come to church Easter Sunday if I'm alive." But he didn't show up.

After the service, the preacher took a lily from the Easter altar, went to the man's home, and knocked on the door. When the man came to the door, the preacher held out the lily and said, "Where's the body?"

—*Larry Eisenberg, Tulsa, Oklahoma*

When I was a student in Theological Seminary at Catholic University in Washington, DC, the first name of one of my fellow students was Bernard, but we all knew him by his nickname, Bunny.

He dropped out of seminary in January, but came back for a visit on Easter Sunday. We were glad to see him again when we spotted him at the church door waiting to greet us as we walked from the church in procession after the Easter service. And, of course, every one of us, as we passed, said to him: "Happy Easter, Bunny!"

—*Rev. Terrence Tully, Spokane, Washington*

I bet any Sunday could be made as popular at church as Easter if you made them into fashion shows too.

—*Will Rogers*

"And the third day he rose again." There is the essential doctrine of which the whole elaborate structure of Christian faith and morals is the only logical consequence. Now we may call it devastating; we may call it revelation, or we may call it rubbish; but if we call it dull, then words have no meaning at all.

—*Dorothy L. Sayers*

Our Lord has written the promise of Resurrection not in books alone but in every leaf of springtime.

—*Martin Luther*

Christianity has died many times and risen again, for it has a God who knows the way out of the grave.

—*G. K. Chesterton*

Let fate do her worst;
There are relics of joy,
Bright dreams of the past,
Which she cannot destroy;
Which come in the night-time
Of sorrow and care.
And bring back the features that joy used to wear.

—*Thomas Moore*

The disciples were filled with joy when they saw the (risen) Lord.

—*John 20:21*

Wendell Berry, in one of his poems, urges us to "Practice Resurrection." It's a strange commands but a true one. The gift of resurrection, God's great triumph over death and meaninglessness—the divine "Yes!" to us—has to be chosen and accepted by us every day.

—**The Anglican Digest**

The editors of The Los Angeles Times *initially declined to run the following Palm Sunday* B.C. *comic strip by Johnny Hart on March 31, 1996, in the paper's comic section because of its religious message. After receiving complaints from some of its readers,* The Times *editors decided to run the Palm Sunday strip and two other* B.C. *strips with Easter themes in the paper's religion section on Saturday, April 6, the day before Easter.*

Ariel Remler, a Times *spokesperson, told* The Joyful Noiseletter, *"We didn't think those comic strips were appropriate for the comic pages for an audience that is so large and diverse."*

Reminded that other nationally syndicated cartoonists also occasionally do a cartoon strip with a religion theme, Remler said: "We respect the affirmation of personal religious faith, but the editors reserve the right to edit. Some religious-themed B.C. *comic strips in the future could appear on the comics pages, or in the religion section."*

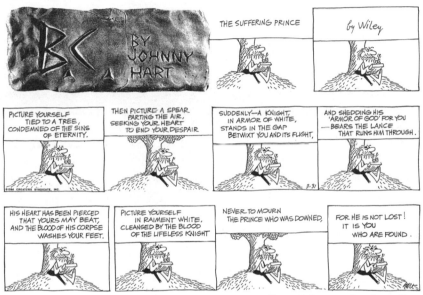

They Lost Their Marbles

"I read Dr. Paul L. Maier's article ("Resurrection of Jesus has never been disproved") in the April *JN* with great interest.

"I am a 46-year-old second-career minister who graduated from the Methodist Theological School of Ohio a year ago. While at seminary, I was often involved with one particular professor who was big into the Jesus Seminar.

"He used to tell us of how the thoughtful scholars would listen to papers about this New Testament text or that, and then vote by placing a red, gray or black marble into a box. Since then, on a few occasions, one of my parishioners has come to me and asked about something done or said by the Jesus Seminar.

"I would tell them about the careful scholarship that went into their semi-annual meetings and about their three-color voting system. I would tell them that after many years, they finally lost their marbles and published their findings."

—*Rev. Ronald B. Hall, Highwater Congregational United Church of Christ, Newark, Ohio*

Laughing at the Grim Reaper

FMC member Carl R. Harfield, M.S., a.k.a. "Doctor Silly," who lives in Evanston, Illinois, took a lighthearted look at death when he turned 82:

"Do I fear death?" he wrote *JN*. "I hope not. Both experiences lie ahead for me, closer than I would like to admit. Like most people, I would prefer an easy passage from this planet to the eternal kingdom.

"Silliness seems most appropriate in preparation to meet the Grim Reaper. We can go out with a funny story or a joke. And a prayer to a loving God who appreciates good humor.

"Think of all the advantages of the next life: no income taxes, no doctors' and dentists' bills, and no waiting in line at supermarkets. Perhaps the greatest bonus will be that one can expect only a few politicians will make it.

"Let's say to death—pfft!"

The Risen Christ by the Sea
Jack Jewell, artist

"The Risen Christ by the Sea" (following), the logo of *The Joyful Noiseletter*, has become a very popular print among Christians of all denominations. Many churches have seen it as a representation of "the Easter laugh"—God's last laugh on the devil when He raised Jesus from the dead—and have reprinted it in their Easter Sunday bulletins. (Full-color prints in various sizes are available from the Fellowship of Merry Christians, PO Box 895, Portage, Michigan 49081-0895. Or call 800-877-2757.)

God's Last Laugh

FMC member Ron Cichowicz, a free-lance writer and communication specialist in Pittsburgh, shared his thoughts on his vision of a smiling, joyful Christ and God's great Easter laugh:

My seven-year-old son asked why he never sees pictures of Jesus laughing. I assured him that a few such artistic renditions do exist—Jack Jewell's "The Risen Christ by the Sea" comes to mind—but admittedly I'm not aware of many.

My answer satisfied my son. But his question still bothers me. Research shows that a sense of humor and the ability to laugh heartily and often are good for you, both physically and mentally. I believe they also are critical to our spiritual well-being.

Imagine what it must have been like for Joseph. On his way home from a hard day in the carpentry shop, a neighbor stops him and says, "I heard about Jesus staying behind at the Temple. I think He should be punished."

Joseph pauses, just long enough to remember Who Jesus' real father is. He winks at Mary: "Maybe you ought to do it."

I suppose we all have favorite images of Jesus. I'm sure some prefer to see Him as teacher, passionately delivering the Sermon on the Mount; others picture Him displaying anger as He routs the money changers from the Temple; still others envision Him in anguish on the cross.

I prefer the Lord smiling, even laughing, because I'm convinced the human side of Jesus could not have endured His public ministry (not to mention the company of His apostles) nor even accepted His crucifixion without a sense of humor.

Of all the places where Jesus could have performed His first miracle, He chose a wedding. No doubt He was surrounded by people laughing and enjoying themselves. Perhaps Jesus danced with His mother—or maybe with a rotund aunt who wouldn't take no for an answer.

When the wine needed replenishing, Jesus could have matter-of-factly told the waiters the urns have been refilled. Instead, He instructs them to fill the urns with water. But wait a minute, fellas, take a look. That's not water in there; it's wine. And not just any wine, but the choicest in the land. Gotcha!

Did Jesus play practical jokes? I don't know, but I'd have loved to have been there when Peter asked Jesus to teach him to walk on water. All goes well for a while . . . Peter's actually doing it . . . he's near the boat . . .

Ker-splash!

I can imagine Jesus unable to resist saying to His soggy Apostle, "You know, Peter, if your faith was just a little stronger . . ."

Or how about the time Jesus was walking and preaching to the masses, only to look up at the diminutive tax collector, Zaccheus, hanging precariously from a tree.

I imagine that even today Jesus delights—not in a mean-spirited way, but with perfect love—in watching us struggle with our human imperfections. Like when we play "Let's Make a Deal" with God: "Lord, let me out of this speeding ticket just this once, and I promise I'll try to get to church every Sunday."

No doubt, many of us who attend church are another source of amusement, sleeping through the sermon, singing off-key enough to make the heavenly hosts cringe, and exchanging the sign of peace so reluctantly that you'd swear everyone in church was wearing a joy buzzer.

What makes me think Jesus has a well-honed sense of humor? A big element of humor is surprise. That's why people laugh when someone slips on a banana peel. They're not being cruel. When someone is walking down the street, we expect them to keep going— not suddenly fly up into the air and land with a thud. What makes that whole scenario funny is the surprise.

In a sense, the "banana peel" of our faith is the empty tomb. Until Jesus came, once people died and were buried, they stayed put. So the "surprise" of Jesus' Resurrection (after some initial fear, panic, and doubt) first brought joy, then good humor, and ultimately laughter to His followers. So it does even today.

As Christians, we know we are destined to have the last laugh. And the joke will be on those who refused to believe.

"Uh oh! I think we turned the wrong way during the processional."

Why Aren't the Horns Blowing?

The news is good! Jesus is alive! The stone is rolled away. Why aren't we shouting—the victory's won!? Why aren't the drums drumming . . .

and the doves flying
and the knees kneeling
and the hands clapping
and the horns blowing
and the tambourines playing
and the bells pealing
and the trumpets blaring
and the cymbals clashing
and the crowds clamoring
and the hearts rejoicing
and the eyes smiling
and the bands marching
and the banners flying
and the voices calling
and the hearts rejoicing
and the tongues praising
and the choirs singing
and the children laughing
and the arms waving
and the bells pealing?

—Anonymous, contributed by FMC member James R. Swanson,
editor of **Pastors Confidential** *in Costa Mesa, California*

Fullness of Joy

Rev. Charles F. Foster, a 75-year-old retired pastor in Wellsboro, Pennsylvania, composed this poem, which he says can be sung to the tune of "What a Friend We Have in Jesus."

Joy that comes in knowing Jesus,
Joy the Spirit brings to me;
For the Spirit glorifies Him;
Takes of Him and shows it me,

Joy that comes in birth from sorrow;
Dark the day of Calvary
Out of death and suffering anguish
Comes the joy of souls set free.

Though disciples sorrowed greatly
And the world rejoiced that day,
Through the Resurrected Savior
Comes the joy none takes away.
Joy abundant, satisfying,
Joys that overflow the brim,
When we ask of God the Father,
And receive it all through Him.

Joy that's based on knowing Jesus'
Incarnation, life, and death,
Resurrection and ascension,
Holy Spirit's living breath.
Oh, the peace in knowing Jesus
In a world of sin and strife;
Victor over all the evil
Of this world through endless life!
　　—John 16:12–33

WORSHIP TAKES OFF WHEN FLIGHT ATTENDANTS USHER

"Punch in with me, if you will, 1 Corinthians, thirteenth chapter . . ."

© 1996 Steve Phelps

FMC member Rev. Paul Lintern, associate pastor at First English Lutheran Church, Mansfield, Ohio, wondered what would happen if a crew of flight attendants took over ushering duties at a local church and wrote the following imaginary scene:

Good morning, ladies and gentlemen, and welcome to United Lutheran Church, worship number ten forty-five. My name is Harold Angel and I am the Chief Ushering attendant for your worship today. It is a pleasure to have you worshiping with us.

Spiritual safety is our number-one priority. Worship attendants are standing in the aisle holding a safety information card. Please take the card out of the pew pocket in front of you and follow along as we cover the important features of this worship model.

If you are sitting in an exit row, you may be required to assist the ushering crew in the event of a spiritual emergency. If you are unable to perform the functions described on the front of the safety card—prayer, plate passing, special music during offering—please advise a worship attendant at the conclusion of these announcements.

For the prelude, please fasten your pewbelt, low and tight across your lap. Worshipers must remain seated when a "fasten pewbelt" symbol appears in your bulletin.

There are eight exit doors on this model 747 worship space—four on each side of the sanctuary. An evacuation slide raft which inflates automatically is located at each door, in case the service runs long and you risk failing to get to the restaurant before the Methodists. Look around and locate the exit closest to your pew. In the event of a rapid recessional, the acolyte will illuminate the signs above each door.

This worship center is equipped with seat cushions, which may be found either under your pew or behind the kneelers. Do not remove the cushion at this time, but if during the service, you find yourself uncomfortable—because of the pew or the sermon—simply remove the cushion from the pouch, slip it under you, and pull down sharply one of the red waist straps. The cushion can also be inflated by blowing into the attached tube.

If it is needed, oxygen is available at several places throughout this worship center. Please see a worship attendant if you need oxygen.

For worship to take off, you must be sitting in an upright position and your pew kneelers must be locked in place. All carry-in items must be securely placed under the pew or in the pew racks, next to the green worship book.

Federal Spirituality Regulations prohibit smoking at any time or any location during this worship service. Tampering with the smoke detector in the narthex lavatories also is prohibited.

Worship Takes Off When Flight Attendants Usher   **99**

Thank you for your attention. We invite you to relax and enjoy the service. Worship attendants are here for your safety and spiritual needs. If we can make your worship experience more meaningful, feel free to call on us.

The senior pastor has informed us that we have been cleared for take-off; we will be on our journey momentarily. Thank you again for worshiping with United Lutheran Church.

IN THE
MARRY MONTH
OF JUNE

"Laura, is there someone else?"

After an unusually busy day that included three weddings followed by a funeral, an exhausted pastor in Indianapolis—at the end of the funeral service—congratulated the widow.

—*Robert J. Stipp, First Baptist Church of Greater Toledo, Holland, Ohio*

On a trip to Gatlinburg, Tennessee, FMC member Sally Dillon, of Timberville, Virginia, and her family stayed in a hotel where author Tim LaHaye was giving a talk on Christian marriage.

In the packed elevator going back to their room that evening, her son asked one of the participants in the LaHaye conference, "What were you learning about in your meeting tonight?"

"I was learning how to make my marriage happier," answered the surprised man.

The boy turned to his mother and exclaimed: "See, Mom! You didn't need to go to those meetings! You and Daddy already knew all the stuff!"

A pastor was called to a local nursing home to perform a wedding. An anxious old man met him at the door. The pastor sat down to counsel the old man and asked several questions. "Do you love her?"

The old man replied, "Nope."

"Is she a good Christian woman?"

"I don't know for sure," the old man answered.

"Does she have lots of money?" asked the pastor.

"I doubt it."

"Then why are you marrying her?" the preacher asked.

"'Cause she can drive at night," the old man said.

—*George Goldtrap, Madison, Tennessee*

A young couple came into the office of Msgr. Charles Dollen of Poway, California, to fill out the prenuptial-questions form. The young man, who had never talked to a priest before, was nervous, and Msgr. Dollen tried to put him at ease.

When they came to the question, "Are you entering this marriage of your own free will?" there was a long pause. Finally, his fiancee looked at the young man and said, "Put down 'Yes.'"

A pastor received the following thank-you note from a newlywed in his congregation: "Dear Pastor: I want to thank you for performing our marriage ceremony. It was beautiful the way you brought my happiness to a conclusion."

—*Pastor Dennis R. Fakes, Lindsborg, Kansas*

Excerpt from a religious tract handed on a street corner to Bishop Frank H. Benning, an FMC member, near St. James Anglican Church in Atlanta, Georgia:

At the age of ten, I had accepted Jesus as my Savior, and had promised God at that time that I would go to Bible College and serve Him, but as a teenager I decided to flirt with the devil and ended up getting married and living in sin instead.

Rev. Estill Franklin, 103, a retired Methodist minister, and Fern Brown, 90, were married on March 29, 1996, in the chapel at the Wesley Manor Retirement Village in Crawfordsville, Indiana. After the ceremony, the newlyweds took a honeymoon ride around town in a limousine and returned to the retirement home for a small reception. Asked their plans for the rest of the day, the bride replied: "A nap. All of this has worn me out."
   —The Indianapolis Star

Men marry women hoping they won't change; women marry men hoping they will.
   —Msgr. Joseph P. Dooley, St. Rocco's Church, Martins Creek,
   Pennsylvania

On their seventh wedding anniversary, John and Jacque McBride of Indianapolis took their two small children to Sunday liturgy at St. Mary's Catholic Church in Danville, Indiana. During petitions, the priest, Fr. Charles Chesebrough, asked children if they wished to offer any prayers.

   Four-year-old Justin McBride raised his hand, intending to ask for prayers for his parents' wedding anniversary, but it came out this way: "I'm praying to Jesus that Mommy and Daddy will get married today."

Grace Presbyterian Church in Wichita, Kansas recently announced a new slogan—"Building Bridges." The following blooper subse-

quently appeared in the church's newsletter: "BUILDING BRIDES . . .WITH GOD ALL THINGS ARE POSSIBLE!"
—*Rev. Warren J. Keating, Derby, Kansas*

FMC member Rev. Mark A. Katrick, pastor of Immanuel United Church of Christ, Zanesville, Ohio, passes on this verbal wedding blooper:

The bride and groom had chosen Mark 10:6–9, and Pastor Katrick dutifully began to read: "But in the beginning, at the time of creation, God made them male and female. As the Scripture says, a man will leave his wife and be united with his mother and father."

When the famous politician and orator William Jennings Bryan (1860–1925) was a young man, he went to the home of the father of his prospective wife to ask him for her hand in marriage. Bryan was determined to impress the father by quoting from the Bible, and he chose this Proverb: "Whosoever findeth a wife findeth a good thing, and obtaineth favor with the Lord."

Bryan was unnerved when the father replied by quoting Paul: "He that marrieth doeth well, but he that marrieth not doeth better."

Bryan, never at a loss for words, said: "Paul had no wife and Solomon had 700. Therefore, I believe Solomon ought to be the better judge as to marriage."
—*Rev. Dennis R. Fakes*

The marriages of couples who harp at each other were not necessarily made in heaven.
—*Catherine Hall, Pittsburgh, Pennsylvania*

Why do brides buy their wedding gowns, and grooms rent their wedding suits?
—*Msgr. Joseph P. Dooley*

The preacher says, "Let no man put asunder," and two-thirds of the married world is asunder in less than three months.
—*Will Rogers*

At a wedding reception attended by four pairs of the divorced and remarried parents and stepparents of the bride and groom, one father rose and gave the following toast to the newlyweds:

I wish you the joy and humor of Jesus, good health, longevity, and only one Christmas every year.

Reprinted with permission of Bil Keane

THE
SPORTS SECTION

The Family Circus

Reprinted with permission of Bil Keane

A short prayer is given before all Southern California College basketball games in Costa Mesa, California. FMC member James R. Swanson, editor of The Pastors Confidential, *reports that Ed Westbrook, assistant to the college president, gave the following pregame prayer recently:*

Heavenly Father, we ask You to bless Your children at play. We do not ask for favoritism. We do not ask for victory for ourselves and defeat for our friends. We do not seek intervention in the borderline calls and bounces of the ball. Keep us from praying piously and then talking trash.

We thank You for the skill and preparation of the players, coaches and especially the referees, without whom all of us fine Christians could not even complete a single game like this without bloodshed. Spare the contestants from injury and the spectators from embarrassing themselves and their school. We ask this in the name of our Lord and Savior, Jesus Christ. Amen.

Basketball Theology

FMC member Pastor Kenneth Pollitz, of New Creation Lutheran Church, Ottawa, Ohio, a former high-school and college basketball player, passed on the following "basketball theology":

Center/forward—Where nobody usually sits on Sunday mornings.
Free throw—A toddler's toss of toys.
Time out—A sermon gone too long.
On the bench—The organist (pianist).
Three-point play—The structure of any good sermon.
Offensive foul—A newly discovered baby's messy diaper.
Ejection—Taking an inconsolable child out of the nursery.
Pre-game warmups—The lighting of the altar candles.
Traveling—Parents walking back and forth with upset children in the back of the church.
Transition game—Movement of people from Sunday school to worship.
Turnover—Exchange of an upset infant between parents. (Also known as the chest pass.)
Opening tip—Suggestion of a short sermon due to the roast in the oven.
Change of possession—The offering.
Fast break—Children coming down for the children's sermon. (Sometimes used to describe the children's movement to the hospitality snacks after worship.)
Slam-dunk—Shorter than usual sermon.
20-second time out—A brief exit to the restrooms.
Rebound—Inspiring special music following a boring sermon.

Any fear is an illusion. You think something is standing in your way, but nothing is really there. What *is* there is an opportunity to do your best and gain some success. If you run into a wall, don't turn around and give up. Figure out how to climb it, go through it, or work around it.

—*Michael Jordan*

"Church attendance has doubled since I had a putting green installed in the vestibule."

"Johnny!" the Sunday school teacher exclaimed. "Remember what happens to little boys who use bad language playing pogs?"

"Sure, teacher," Johnny answered. "They grow up and play golf."

—*Joe Maher, Oxnard, California*

Playing a round of golf with friends, a priest missed the ball several times, then hit it into the rough. He closed his eyes and spat.

"That was a fine thing you did, Father," one of his friends said. "You set an example for us. You used no profanity."

"True," the priest said, "but where I spit no grass will ever grow."

—*Joe Maher*

"Father," a man asked during his confession, "is it a sin to play golf on Sunday?"

"My son, the way you play it's a sin any day," the priest replied.

—*Joe Maher*

Many men play golf religiously—every Sunday.

—*Jim Reed,* **The Funny Side of Golf**

A solemn friend of my grandfather used to go for walks on Sunday, carrying a prayer book, without the least intention of going to church. And he calmly defended it by saying, "I do it, Chessie, as an example to others."

Few modern men, however false, would dare to be so brazen. And I am not sure he was not really a more genuine fellow than the modern man who says vaguely that he has doubts or hates sermons, when he only wants to go and play golf.

—*G. K. Chesterton*

The idea for permanent seat licenses—whereby professional football teams charge a one-time fee of hundreds of thousands of dollars for the right to buy a season ticket forever—has been traced back to a Presbyterian church in Nashville, Tennessee, in 1885. The curator of the Tennessee State Museum reports that members of the First Presbyterian Church (now Downtown Presbyterian Church in Nashville) paid $25 for a choice pew for a six month period, according to the *Decatur* (Illinois) *Herald & Review.*

Competition is everywhere and in single portions is healthy, but in many cases it's overemphasized and leads to the fatal attitude that "winning is everything." My five-year-old nephew, David, gave me a sermon illustration that keeps things in perspective:

After David played in a soccer game, his father asked him, "Hey, David, did you win?"

"I think so," the boy said.

"Well, what was the score, son?" his father asked.

"Six!" the boy replied.

—*FMC member Rev. Dave Fortuna, Lea Joyner Memorial United Methodist Church, Monroe, Louisiana*

© 1996 Ed Sullivan

Reporting on Cal Ripken, the Baltimore Oriole shortstop who broke Lou Gehrig's record for playing in consecutive games, *Time* magazine noted that, unlike other ballplayers, Ripken "has never sulked, maligned, strutted, whined, wheedled, or referred to himself in the third person." On a rare occasion, after umpire Drew Coble threw Ripken out of a game for arguing a call, Coble remarked: "I felt like I was throwing God out of church."

After several years of not having a pro football team in St. Louis, we got the Rams last year. Sunday worship attendance at our church, St. Mark Presbyterian Church in Ballwin, dropped by about an average of fifty on home game days. An average of about ten Rams fans returned to the flock's Sunday worship services after Pastor Howard Gleason inserted the following whimsical announcement in the church bulletin:

"YOU WON'T LOOK SHEEPISH IN RAMS CLOTHING: If you are headed to a Rams football game on a Sunday, please feel free to come to worship in whatever clothing you're wearing to the game. We share in the excitement of having professional football in St. Louis. We also know that noon games make a close time bind for someone going to the game. To make a full day of your Sunday before football, start it off with worship."

Pastor Gleason might have added: "The Rams (8-8) also can use your prayers."

—FMC member Bruce Stombach of Ellisville, Missouri

"Dad, I don't know how you ever did it. Prepare two messages, a Bible study, a Sunday school lesson and keep up with the Cowboys without a VCR!"

© 1996 Steve Phelps

On the feast of Christ the King (the last Sunday before Advent), Fr. William A. Lau of Blessed Trinity Catholic Church in St. Petersburg, Florida, began his homily with a quiz for the congregation. After asking who were "The King of Swing," "The King of Rock," and "The King of the Wild Frontier," the priest asked: "Who was 'The King of the Cowboys'?"

Most of the congregation replied, "Roy Rogers." But a little boy in the front row shouted, "Emmett Smith!"

What Happens to Fishermen Who Lie When They Die?

The Funny Side of Golf *author and FMC member Jim Reed, of Cotter, Arkansas, has written another entertaining book called* The Funny Side of Fishing, *which includes humorous anecdotes, tall tales, and one-liners about Sunday fishermen and pastors. Here are some of them, reprinted with Reed's permission (© 1996 Jim Reed):*

"We should get some of the Sunday morning fishing crowd today."

A devout, churchgoing father was trying to teach his son that lying is a sin and that he shouldn't lie about fishing and other things.

"Do you know what happens to fishermen who lie when they die?" he asked.

The son quickly replied, "They lie still!"

The preacher at the wedding was an ardent fisherman and forgetful. He asked the groom, "Do you promise to love, honor, and cherish this woman?"

"I do," said the groom meekly.

"Okay," said the minister, turning to the bride, "reel him in!"

Sitting still and wishing
Made no person great;
The good Lord sends the fishing,
but you must dig the bait.

An answer to this question
Is what I greatly wish;
Does fishing make men liars—
Or do only liars fish?
　　　—*Author Unknown*

© 1996 Doc Goodwin

Johnny was on his way home one Sunday evening with a full string of catfish when he saw the town's preacher approaching him. Since there was no way to escape, Johnny walked up to the minister and said, "Reverend, see what these catfish got for biting worms on Sunday."

The new minister looked at Jake Bratwurst and said, "I'm told you went to the ball game instead of church this morning."

"That's a lie," snapped Jake. "And here's the string of fish to prove it."

When the preacher approached the boy who was fishing in the park pond, he said, "Young man do you know the parables?"

"Yes sir," the lad quickly replied.

"Which do you like best?"

The boy looked up and, grinning, replied, "The one where everybody loafs and fishes."

While shoveling snow, two long-time fishing buddies discussed how long it had been since they were ice fishing together. "What do you say, George?" one said. "Let's get our poles and saw and go one more time."

"I'm game," replied the other, shivering a little at the very thought of it.

As they prepared to cut the hole, a voice said, "There ain't no fish under this ice." Startled by the eerie voice, the two looked all around them, but no one was in sight.

As they touched saw to ice again, they heard once more, "There ain't no fish under this ice."

"That can't be God," said one, "because it's a woman's voice and besides she uses poor English."

The other fisherman yelled, "Who are you?"

"I'm not God," came the answer, "I'm just the manager of this ice skating rink."

Two men, fishing on Sunday morning, were feeling guilty. Said one, "I suppose we should have stayed home and gone to church."

The other replied, "Heck, I couldn't have gone to church anyway. My wife's in bed with the flu."

A fellow quit going fishing on Sunday and began going to church. The preacher, grateful to see him, said, "Henry, it makes me feel good to see you and your wife here every Sunday."

"Well," said the fisherman, "I figured I'd rather hear your sermon than hers."

A fellow isn't thinking mean—out fishing.
His thoughts are mostly clean—out fishing
He doesn't knock his fellow men
Or harbor any grudges then.
A fellow's at his finest when—out fishing.

The rich are comrades to the poor—out fishing.
All brothers of a common core—out fishing.
The urchin with the pin and string
Can chum with millionaire and king.
Vain pride is a forgotten thing—out fishing.

A feller's glad to be a friend—out fishing.
A helpful hand he'll always lend—out fishing.
The brotherhood of rod and line,
And sky and stream is always fine.
Men come real close to God's design—out fishing.
        —Author Unknown

A bass fisherman looked up at the storm clouds over head and said to his fishing partner, "Probably the last completely accurate weather forecast was when God told Noah there was a 100 percent chance of precipitation."

A Sunday school teacher said, "Johnny, do you think Noah did a lot of fishing when he was on the Ark?"

"Naw," replied Johnny, "How could he, with just two worms?"

Noah said to his wife: "Do me a favor, and stop saying, 'Into each life a little rain must fall.'"

Since about three-fourths of the earth's surface is water and about one-fourth land, it stands to reason that the good Lord intended for man to spend three times as much time fishing as he does plowing.

© 1996 Goddard Sherman

Any man who can swap horses or catch fish, and not lie about it, is just about as pious as men ever get to be in this world.
—*Josh Billings*

It's against the law to catch fish in some waters and a miracle in others.

We may say of angling as Dr. Boteler said of strawberries: "Doubtless God could have made a better berry, but doubtless God never did." And so, (if I might be judge) God never did make a more calm, quiet innocent recreation than angling.
—*Izaak Walton*

Fishing is not a matter of life and death. It is much more important than that.

Presidents have only two moments of personal seclusion. One is in prayer; the other is fishing—and they cannot pray all the time!
—*Herbert Hoover*

For 20 years or so, the average fisherman's mother asks him where he is going. For the next 40 years, his wife asks him the same question. And then, at his funeral, the mourners wonder the same thing

"Would you be upset if I told you that, while you were getting ready, I've been to church and back?"

© 1996 Ed Sullivan

A Fisherman's Prayer

God grant that I may live to fish until my dying day
And when my final cast is made
And life has slipped away,
I pray that God's great landing net

Will catch me in its sweep
And in His mercy, God will judge me
Big enough to keep
   —Author unknown

Where Did All the Men Go?

After reading several articles in both Catholic and Protestant publications lamenting the phenomenon of men disappearing from churches, I decided to talk with my Guardian Angel, Symeon. Symeon has a sense of humor, and always cheers me up when I'm perplexed.

"Symeon," I asked, "How do we get American men back to church?"

Symeon heaved a heavy sigh. "The Boss tells us to keep trying to get them back, but we find them everywhere except in church. But the Boss has never been a pessimist and sees some signs of hope."

Symeon told me he had just returned from a Promise Keepers convention at the Silverdome in Pontiac, Michigan, home of the Detroit Lions. "It was odd—so many Christians gathering in the home of the Lions," he said. "I was astonished to see 70,000 men of all denominations—Protestants, Catholics, Orthodox—praying and singing and praising the Boss. It's been a long time—centuries, in fact—since I heard so many men saying nice things about the Boss. Someone even offered to sell me a Promise Keepers T-shirt and an angel pin.

"Wow, was it noisy in that football stadium! Nobody ever rooted for the Detroit Lions like that, even when they were winning 50 years ago. You know, those Detroit Lions really need prayers. The Detroit Tigers do too, for that matter.

"But I was happy to see pastors of all denominations reaching out to bring men back to church. We hope Promise Keepers will instruct and equip men to commit themselves to their wives, children, families, and churches.

"I've got a suggestion," Symeon added. "There ought to be a Promise Keepers for women too. It takes two to keep a promise, after all."

Symeon paused a moment, then said: "They'll get more men to come to church when the churches stop depicting the Lord Jesus as a sad-sack wimp and start portraying Him as the most joyful, loving, balanced, triumphant, and manly of men, who bravely challenged the pagan culture of His times and sacrificed Himself so that all men and women might have life."

—*Cal Samra*

EASY ON THE ALLELUIAS, HARRY

"Tom, I'm not crazy about the direction you seem to be taking with our choir."

How do you guard against Satan? Laughter, writes the Rev. J. Stephen Hines, pastor of St. Luke's Episcopal Church in Asheville, North Caro-

lina, in the forward to his new book, Easy on the Alleluias, Harry. *Rev. Hines quotes C. S. Lewis'* Screwtape Letters, *in which the devil counsels his protégé, Screwtape: "Christians who laugh are poor prospects."*

Acclaimed by former President George Bush, who is a member of St. Martin's Episcopal Church in Houston, Texas, Rev. Hines' book is a collection of Episcopal church humor. Here are a few samples:

Coming through the church just before the service was scheduled to begin, a bishop noted with some displeasure that there was a very sparse congregation.

"There are not many people in church today," the bishop said to the rector. "Did you tell them I was coming?"

"No, bishop," the rector replied. "Someone else must have."

"But you have to go to church. You're the pastor."

© 1989 Dennis Daniel, *Brother Blooper*

During a children's sermon, a priest asked the youngsters, "Does anyone know what a bishop does?"

A young lad raised his hand. "Moves diagonally."

For those who are to preach, it is customary in my country that the preacher kneel for prayer before entering the pulpit. The daughter of one of my clergy noticed her father praying Sunday after Sunday as he prepared to mount the pulpit. She asked her daddy what he prayed for. The priest replied that he was asking God to help him preach a better sermon, whereupon the child asked, "Well, why doesn't He?"

—Archbishop Desmond Tutu of South Africa

"I kept hoping my problem would turn up on Donahue, Oprah, Montel, Ricki or Maury, but when it didn't, I decided to see you."

© 1996 Ed Sullivan

. . . If You Do . . . If You Don't

If a pastor preaches over 12 minutes, he's a windbag; if his sermon is short, he came unprepared.

If he gives his sermon in a quiet voice, he's a bore; if he puts feeling into his sermon, he's too emotional.

If the church budget is balanced, he's a good businessman; if he asks for money to balance the budget, he's greedy.

If he visits church members in their homes, he's nosy; if he doesn't, he's a snob and doesn't care.

If he's young, he's not experienced; if he's old, he should retire.

If he lives, the pastor at the church down the block is a better preacher and counselor than he is; if he dies, there was nobody like him and his equal will never be seen again.

—From a New Zealand church newsletter

Pastor's Prayer

Heavenly Father, I truly believe in the fruits of the Holy Spirit, but please tell me: What should I do with those two lemons in my church choir?

—Hal Wickliffe, Harrison, New York

"What do you think of the video I made of your sermon last Sunday?"

© 1996 Goddard Sherman

Sure, it cost more, but Pastor Lou enjoyed staying home while sending the *congregation* on vacation.

The Reverend Dennis R. Fakes overheard this conversation:

"What do you believe about God?"

"I believe what my church teaches and believes."

"And what does your church teach and believe?"

"My church teaches and believes what I believe."

"What do you and your church believe?"

"Oh, we believe exactly the same thing."

My pastor, Rev. Joe Wilson, a Nazarene in Mount Pleasant, Texas, preached a sermon, "The Unknown Depths of Sin." He quoted old Brother Jones, who said to a fellow preacher after a particularly bad sermon, "I believe you can go the deepest, and stay the longest, and come up with the least of anyone I've ever seen."

—*Chaplain Donald E. Sides, Mount Pleasant, Texas*

On his very first day in office, a new pastor got a call from his predecessor. He congratulated him on his new charge and told him that in the center drawer of his desk he had left three envelopes, all numbered, which he was to open in order when he got into trouble.

After a short-lived honeymoon with the congregation, the heat began to rise and the minister decided to open the first envelope. His predecessor advised him: "Blame me for the problem. After all, I'm long gone and have problems of my own; and if it will help, point out my shortcomings as the reason things are bad."

That worked for a while, but then things got sour again. The pastor opened the second envelope, which read: "Blame the denomination. They're big and rich. They can take it."

That worked well for a while, but then the storm clouds gathered again, and in desperation the pastor went to the drawer and opened the third envelope. It said: "Prepare three envelopes."

—*FMC member Rev. Ronald H. Weinelt of McDonough, Georgia, founder of the Association of Battered Clergy*

"Mother and I have loved having you here all these years, son. But if you think this new degree in theology is finally 'it' for you, we'd like to rent your room."

A Prayer for Your Pastor

Lord, let me be a pillar of strength to hold him up, and not a thorn in his flesh to sap his strength, nor a burden on his back to pull him down. Let me support him without striving to possess him. Let me lift his hands without placing shackles around them. Let me give him help that he may devote more time in working for the salvation of others and less time in gratifying my vanity. Let me work for him as the minister of all the members, and not compel him to spend precious time bragging on me. Let me strive to be happy as he serves me less and others more. Amen.

    —*from* **The Anglican Digest**

WHAT IF GOD HAD AN ANSWERING MACHINE?

"For a church service schedule, press one. For office hours, press two. For the forgiveness of sins, press three. If you want to pray alone, hang up."

© 1996 M. Larry Zanco

FMC member Rev. Paul Kummer, of Grace Lutheran Church in Destin, Florida, wrote the following as he mused on what would happen if God decided to install an answering machine:

Imagine praying and hearing this: "Thank you for calling My Father's House. Please select one of the following four options: Press 1 for a request. Press 2 for a thanksgiving. Press 3 to complain. For all other inquiries, press 4."

So you press 1 and hear: "We're sorry. All of the angels are helping other customers right now. Please stay on the line. Your call will be answered in the order it was received."

What would it be like if you heard the following responses as you called God's answering machine?

"To receive the latest promotional gift with your order from Paradise Parlor, press 0, and an operator will assist you.

"To find out how many angels dance on the head of a pin, press 5.

"If you'd like King David to sing a psalm for you, press 6.

"To find out if your relative is here, enter his/her date of death and listen for the list that follows.

"For reservation information or to confirm your reservations at My Father's House, press the letters J-O-H-N, followed by the numbers 3-1-6.

"To know what your pastor is doing at this moment, press 7.

"For answers to nagging questions about dinosaurs, the age of the earth, and where Noah's Ark is, wait till you get here!

"If you want to know what I think of American politics, don't press anything. Hang up and listen for laughter.

"Our computers show that you have called once today already. Please hang up immediately.

"This office is closed for the weekend. Please call again Monday."

Thank God you can't call Him too often. You only need to ring once and He hears you. Because of Jesus, you never get a busy signal. God takes each call personally. He knows each caller personally: *"Then you will call and the Lord will answer; you will cry for help, and he will say: Here am I"* (Isaiah 58:9).

Moreover, God often calls us. Are you waiting for His call, or will your answering machine talk to Him? If you listen carefully, you will hear music in the background and God singing, "I just called to say 'I love you! I just called to say how much I care . . .'"

What If God Had an Answering Machine?   **129**

"It may seem impersonal, but it's improved my answers to prayers two-hundred percent."

STEWARD:
A KEEPER
OF PIGS

I just discovered something about myself: I am "a keeper of pigs"—etymologically speaking, that is.

As a Christian, I am a steward. The word *steward* comes from the Old English word *stiweard,* which was made up of *sty* (a pen for pigs) and *weard* (a ward of a keeper). A *stiweard* took care of the lord of the manor's pigs, overseeing everything from their health and feeding to their protection and breeding. When the steward returned the pigs to the manor lord, he had to account for his care of the animals, or his stewardship.

All of life is a matter of stewardship. Someday I will have to give an account to the ultimate Lord of the Manor, the Lord God, who owns everything.

—*Rev. Carl Marks,* **United Church of Christ Congregational, Arcade, New York**

Once a year, strange creatures in quaint costumes pop into our lives. Sticking out their hands palm upward, or opening little sacks, they ask us to dig into our stores of goodies. And they threaten all kinds of nastiness if we aren't forthcoming. I'm speaking, of course, about the fall stewardship campaign. Trick or treat!

—*Rev. Ruth Eller,* **The Anglican Digest**

If the widow's mite had been invested 2,000 years ago in the First National Bank of Jerusalem, at 4 percent interest, compounded semiannually, the $4,800,000,000,000,000,000,000,000 now in the account could pay off several national debts.

—*Rev. Felix A. Lorenz Jr., Northville, Michigan*

"We'll have to be more generous with our contributions if we want to build the rest of the church."

Flat Tithe Plan

FMC member James R. Swanson, editor of *The Pastor's Confidential* in Costa Mesa, California, has proposed a simple plan, which he says will solve the financial problems of churches, enabling them to increase their pastors' salaries, pay off church mortgages, double missions giving, and eliminate all fundraising projects and special appeals.

Swanson calls it the flat tithe plan: Every Christian, regardless of income, would simply give the church a flat 10 percent of his or her earnings.

"I wonder why someone hasn't thought of that before?" he wonders.

Pardon the pun, but it Costa Mesa money to run a church these days.

"Ten percent might be adequate for God, but we here at First National prefer 18 percent."

Before leading a worship service with a Disciples of Christ minister, *JN* consulting editor Rev. Dennis R. Fakes, a Lutheran pastor in Lindsborg, Kansas, asked the minister if he wanted to wear a surplice (a white vestment).

"Surplice!" he exclaimed. "I'm a Disciple. What do I know about surplices? All I know about is deficits."

Some go to church to weep, while others go to sleep.
Some go to tell their woes, others to show their clothes.
Some go to hear the preacher, others like the solo screecher.
Boys go to reconnoiter, girls go because they orter.
Many go for good reflections, precious few to help collections.
   —*Joe Maher, Oxnard, California*

FMC member Bruce H. Burnside of Rockville, Maryland, went to worship at the Washington National Cathedral one Sunday morning. Just before the collection plates were passed, the Very Reverend Nathan D. Baxter, dean of the Cathedral, stood and announced, smiling broadly, "The water of salvation is free, but it costs for the plumbing."

The pastor of a small church exhorted his flock to give generously when the collection plate was passed. "Give," he pleaded, "as though it were going right back into your own pocket."

After the service, the pastor chided one of the members: "George, I noticed that you let the collection plate go right by you in spite of my appeal."

"Well, Reverend," the man replied, "I figured as long as the money was going back into my pocket anyway, it didn't need no round trip."

—*Orville H. Griffin,* **Ohio Baptist Messenger**

© 1996 Dennis Daniel

In the early days of our country, an old Quaker was shopping in town when a runaway team of horses destroyed a vegetable vendor's cart. Many people began to tell the vendor how sorry they were that this had happened. The old Quaker took off his hat and put five dollars in it. "I'm sorry, five dollars," he said, and began passing the hat around.

As followers of Jesus the Christ, our expressions of love and sympathy must come in concrete action and not just words.

—*Rev. Larry Lea Odom-Groh,* **The Christian Pioneer,** *First Christian Church, Chillicothe, Missouri*

"Sure, I believe it's more blessed to give than to receive. But you're taking it out of context."

© 1996 Goddard Sherman

One Sunday in church a little boy took off his tie and put it into the offering plate.

"What are you doing?" asked his mother.

"What the minister said," answered the little boy. "He told us to give our ties and offerings."

—*Timothy Roland, Gillette, New Jersey*

A pastor asked a youngster: "Johnny, do you know where little boys go if they don't put their money in the collection plate?"

"Yes, pastor," the boy answered. "They go to the movies."

—*George Goldtrap, Madison, Tennessee*

After church one Sunday, a pastor's five-year-old daughter asked him why people put their money in collection plates. The pastor explained that everything we have comes from God and that what people give is returning some of it to God.

"Well," she replied after a thoughtful silence, "if God needs more, why doesn't He just make some more?"

—*Jim Johnson, Abilene, Texas*

A young girl wrote in her church grade school: "Syntax is all the money collected at church from sinners."

—*Catherine Hall, Pittsburgh, Pennsylvania*

I think that I shall never see
A church that's all it ought to be.
A church whose members never stray
Beyond the straight and narrow way.
A church that has no empty pews,
Whose people all pay their dues.
A church whose members always sing,
And flock to church when bells ring.
Such perfect churches there may be,
But none of them are known to me.
But still we'll work and pray and plan
To make our own the best we can.

—*Msgr. Joseph P. Dooley, St. Rocco's*
Church, Martins Creek, Pennsylvania

STEWARDSHIP ONE-LINERS

When it comes to giving, some folks stop at nothing.

—*Mary Ann Herman, El Paso, Texas*

If one first gives himself to the Lord, all other giving is easy.

—*Robert E. Harris, Asheville, North Carolina*

The smart charitable person gives 'til it hurts, except for advice.
—*Mary Ann Herman, El Paso, Texas*

If you let God take the foremost, you won't have to worry about the devil taking the hindmost.

Americans spend fifteen times more money gambling than they donate to churches.
—*Rev. Denny J. Brake, Raleigh, North Carolina*

"I've stirred up their sense of moral responsibility. Now go out and hit 'em with some funny stuff on tithing and stewardship."

© 1995 Ed Sullivan

Steward: A Keeper of Pigs **137**

WITTY ONE-LINERS

© 1995 Jonny Hawkins

The Lord created the world in six days and rested on the seventh. On the eighth day, He started answering complaints.

—*Gene Brown*

Some people are kind, polite, and sweet-spirited—until you try to get into their pew.
—George Goldtrap, Madison, Tennessee

Many folks want to serve God, but only as advisers.
—Sr. Monique Rysavy, Owatonna, Minnesota

It is easier to preach ten sermons than it is to live one.
—Rev. Robert E. Harris

A conservative thinks children ought to pray in school; a liberal thinks children ought to ride a bus to school; and a moderate thinks children ought to pray on the bus.
—Jim Reed, **A Treasury of Ozark Country Humor**

The good Lord didn't create anything without a purpose, but the fly comes close.
—Mark Twain

A Bible that is falling apart probably belongs to someone who isn't.
—Rev. Christian Johnson, Milton, Florida

Most of us spend the first six days of each week sowing wild oats, then we go to church on Sunday and pray for a crop failure.
—Fred Allen

Do you know the three times that most people are in church? When they are hatched, matched, or dispatched.
—Lowell B. Yoder, Holland, Ohio

When you get to your wit's end, you'll find God lives there.
—Elizabeth Yates

Quit griping about your church; if it was perfect, you couldn't belong.
    —*Msgr. Joseph P. Dooley, Martins Creek, Pennsylvania*

Asked once why so many Christians seem much less than perfect, C. S. Lewis replied, "You should have seen them *before* they became Christians."

People are funny. They want the front of the bus, the middle of the road, and the back of the church.
    —*Catherine Hall, Pittsburgh, Pennsylvania*

Outside of traffic, there is nothing that has held this country back as much as committees.
    —*Will Rogers*

Americans are so tense and keyed up that it's impossible even to put them to sleep with a sermon.
    —*Norman Vincent Peale*

My father used to say, "You must have a terrible conscience if you can't sleep in church."
    —*George Goldtrap*

The phrase that is guaranteed to wake up an audience: "And in conclusion."
    —*Charles J. Milazzo, St. Petersburg, Florida*

If a church wants a better pastor, it can get one by praying for the one it has.
    —*Rev. Robert E. Harris*

The person who walks with God is happier than the one who rides in a limousine without Him.
—*Rev. Denny Brake, Raleigh, North Carolina*

Opportunity knocks only once, but temptation bangs on your door for years.
—*Anonymous*

An Episcopalian who decided to read the Bible was surprised to find how often it quoted the Prayer Book.
—*Very Rev. Nathan D. Baxter, Dean, Washington Cathedral*

The road to hell is paved with good conventions.
—*George Goldtrap*

A lot of church members who are singing "Standing on the Promises" are just sitting on the premises.
—*Sr. Monique Rysavy*

We were called to be witnesses, not lawyers.
—*Donna Maddux Cooper, Stillwater, Oklahoma*

There are ten church members by inheritance for one by conviction.
—*Eugene O'Neill*

The purpose of a sermon is to drive home the point, not the congregation.
—*Rev. Denny Brake*

I wonder what would happen if we all agreed to read one of the Gospels until we came to a place that told us to do something, and then went out to do it!
—*James F. Colaianni,* **Apple Seeds**

Every evening I turn my troubles over to God—He's going to be up all night anyway.
    —*Donald J. Morgan, Columbus, Ohio*

Ecumenical agreements are remarkable because theologians love disagreement and are terrified by consensus.
    —*Sir Henry Chadwick, Church of England ecumenist*

One of a pastor's toughest jobs is training sheep to be shepherds.
    —*Rev. Denny Brake*

If you don't like the bleatings of sheep, you shouldn't be a shepherd.
    —*Rev. Felix A. Lorenz, Jr., Northville, Michigan*

Old preachers never die; they just get put out to pastor.
    —*Pastor Dave Buuck, Cambridge, Minnesota*

I don't know how old I am because the goat ate the Bible that had my birth certificate in it. The goat lived to be twenty-seven.
    —*Satchel Paige*

I don't know why some people change churches—what difference does it make which one you stay home from?
    —*Rev. Denny Brake*

A lie is an abomination unto the Lord and a very present help in time of trouble.
    —*Adlai Stevenson*

Not only are the sins of the fathers visited upon the children, but nowadays the sins of the children are visited upon their fathers.
    —*Herbert V. Prochnow, Sr.*

He who lives in a glass house should not invite over he who is without sin.

—*Rev. Lewis Kujawski, St. Elmo, Illinois*

Sometimes when I'm celebrating mass, I feel like the only one who is celebrating.

—*Fr. Martin Wolter, OFM, St. Louis, Missouri*

General Ulysses S. Grant once asked Henry Ward Beecher: "Why does a little fault in a clergyman attract more notice than a great fault in a bad man?"

Replied Beecher: "Perhaps it is for the same reason that a slight stain on a white garment is more readily noticed than a large stain on a colored one."

Nowadays, when someone asks me, "Are you still an Episcopalian?" I have a ready answer: "Yes, very still."

—*Columnist William Murchison*

God Himself does not propose to judge a man till he is dead. So why should I?

—*Samuel Johnson*

If a Savior leaves you as you are and where you are, from what has He saved you?

—*Pastor Denny Brake*

These days so many preachers, it seems, are endlessly quoting psychologists, but have you ever heard a psychologist quote a preacher?

—*Brother Zorba*

Young man, the secret of my success is that at an early age I discovered I was not God.
—*Oliver Wendell Holmes, Jr.*

Pastors can learn a little about timing and relating from good comics.
—*William Willimon*

To make a long story short, don't tell it.
—*Tal Bonham*

Some people just can't enjoy life; the first half of their lives are spent blaming their troubles on their parents and the second half on their children.
—*Rev. Dennis R. Fakes*

Some people think that the Great Commission is what the real estate agent gets when their house is sold.
—*James R. Swanson,* **The Pastors Confidential**

The Toronto Blessing (where people laugh uncontrollably in church) is the answer to every comedian's prayer—getting big laughs when there ain't nothing funny.
—*Burt Rosenberg, Messianic comedian, Arlington, Virginia*

What a good thing Adam had: When he said a good thing, he knew nobody had said it before.
—*Mark Twain*

A single mouse is miracle enough to convert a trillion infidels.
—*Walt Whitman*

"You have to admit, our devotions are more regular since I built it."

© 1992 Ed Koehler

If your left hand doesn't know what your right hand is doing, you should consider running for a job in Washington.

—*Anonymous*

A fanatic is one who is sure the Almighty would agree with him, if only the Almighty had all the facts.

—*Rev. Robert E. Harris,* **Laugh with the Circuit Rider**

To err is human; to blame it on somebody else is even more human.

—*John Nadeau, Medford, Massachusetts*

If it really is religion with these nudist colonies, they sure must turn atheists in the wintertime.

—*Will Rogers*

Dying is easy; comedy is hard.
   —*Groucho Marx*

Some minds are like concrete, thoroughly mixed up and permanently set.
   —*Rev. Denny J. Brake*

All this tooth and claw stuff (in modern litigation) is hard on morals. But then, joylessness just might be endemic to a life at the bar.
   —*Law Professor Maurice Kelman, Wayne State University*

"As we dedicate our daughter to God, we ask you to join us in her spiritual nurture . . . and, if you can, to help contribute to her college fund."

The older we grow, the greater becomes our wonder at how much ignorance one can contain without bursting one's clothes.
   —*Mark Twain*

It ain't so much the things we don't know that get us in trouble. It's the things we know that ain't so.
—*Artemus Ward, American humorist (1867)*

One of the great problems with psychiatry as a helping science is that one often gets started in psychiatry slightly cracked and ends up being totally broke.
—*Rev. Dennis Fakes*

The minimum outpatient treatment for killjoys was prescribed by W.C. Fields: "Start each day with a smile, and get it over with."
—*Fr. John H. Hampsch, CMF, Claretian Tape Ministry, Los Angeles, California*

Anything I can do, we can do better.
—*Rev. Denny Brake*

Peace starts with a smile.
—*Mother Teresa*

CHRISTMAS CHEER

The Family Circus

"Shall I play for you, pa-rum-pa-pum-pummm . . . ?"

Reprinted with permission of Bil Keane

It is good to be children sometimes, and never better than at Christmas when its mighty Founder was a child Himself.
   —*Charles Dickens*

Artist Jan Peters of Chicopee, Massachusetts, unearthed this excerpt from an old Christmas sermon by Anthony of Padua (1195-1231):

Today God made the glorious virgin laugh, because from her is born our laughter. Laughter is born, Christ is born! Therefore, let us laugh and rejoice with the blessed virgin because God has given us in her a cause for laughing and rejoicing.

FMC member Rev. James M. Evans, Jr., pastor of Congress Street United Methodist Church in Lafayette, Indiana, reports that he recently discovered "an ancient Latin text on the banks of the Wabash River":

Gloria in excelsis Deo, et in terra pax et hilaritas hominibus. ("Glory to God in the highest, and on earth peace and hilarity among people.")

Reading the Sunday Scripture on the coming of the Wise Men from Matthew 2:11, a deacon said, "And they presented Him gifts of gold, frankincense, and mirth."

There were only a few shepherds at the first Bethlehem. The ox and the ass understood more of the first Christmas than the high priests in Jerusalem. And it is the same today.

—*Thomas Merton,* **The Seven Storey Mountain**

The Wise Men were truly wise men. Unlike most men, they stopped to ask for directions.

—*George E. Franke, director of pastoral care, Victory Memorial Hospital, Waukegan, Illinois*

Sign seen in a department store: "Make This a Christmas Your Spouse Won't Forget. Charge Everything."

Blooper in a church Christmas bulletin: "The choir will sing 'I Heard the Bills on Christmas Day.'"

I bought my Christmas cards last January. I just can't find them.
—*Erma Bombeck*

FMC member Rev. Dr. K. Geoff Pankhurst, pastor of the Uniting Church in Orange, Australia, visited an orphanage in Pattaya, Thailand, founded by Fr. Raymond Brennan, a Redemptorist priest. Dr. Pankhurst and his wife were there in September, so were surprised to find Fr. Brennan playing Christmas carols.

Dr. Pankhust reported: "Fr. Brennan said that Christmas is too important to celebrate for only a few weeks. He plays carols all year, and some of his influence must have rubbed off on the McDonald's restaurant in Pattaya because they were also playing Christmas carols in September!"

The Family Circus

"It's a Christmas present from God!"

Reprinted with permission of Bil Keane

And a decree went out from Caesar Disgustus that all the post offices should ignore Christmases.
—*Rev. Denny J. Brake, Raleigh, North Carolina*

Our youngest daughter, Nancy, was almost four. My wife and I and our four older children had tried to prepare Nancy for Christmas by talking with her about the real meaning of Christmas and why the family celebrated it.

Nancy had a wonderful Christmas with a lot of presents and toys. A few days later, she was talking with her older sister about what a great Christmas she had, and said, "I sure hope Joseph and Mary have another baby."
—*Donald W. Dugan, Captiva, Florida*

The first-grade class presented a Nativity play shortly before Christmas. When Joseph came to the inn and asked if there was room at the inn, the little boy playing the innkeeper replied, "You're lucky. We just had a cancellation."
—*George Goldtrap, Madison, Tennessee*

During the children's sermon on the third Sunday in Advent at First Baptist Church in Gainesville, Florida, the youth minister remarked: "Bethlehem was a real small town. In fact, it was so small, I'll bet they didn't even have a Pizza Hut."

One young lad quickly and seriously remarked, "Maybe they had a Little Caesar's!"
—*Pastor Lynwood Walters, First Baptist Church, Gainesville, Florida*

"Dear Santa: Last Christmas I asked you for a baby sister. This Christmas I want you to take her back." Robert

One Christmas, I was talking with my four children about the orphan boy our family supported. I told them that he lived in the little village of Bet Sahour, which means "Shepherds' field," near Bethlehem, and attended a Lutheran school.

The kids were wide-eyed to think the school could be located at the very spot where the angels declared good tidings of great joy— all the kids, that is, except my daughter Amy. Her comment: "Figures they'd mess it up with a school!"
—*Clint Kelly, Everett, Washington*

The Family Circus

"I'm very tired, Mommy. Will you say
good night to Jesus for me and
tell him I went to bed?"

Every year in The Joyful Noiseletter's *Christmas issue,* JN *consulting editor Rev. David R. Francoeur, pastor of Christ Episcopal Church in Valdosta, Georgia, offers special Christmas gift suggestions for clergy from the catalog of Balmy Clergy Supply, Inc. Here are a few of the ads:*

Balmy Parrot Concordance

You may have seen all the ads for computerized Bible concordances to assist clergy in preparing sermons. Balmy has a better idea. We've procured and trained many fine parrots as **LIVING CONCORDANCES.** Each parrot has been painstakingly taught a large collection of verses from the Bible and trained to respond to key words. These exceptional birds also make better companions than computer disks. Supply limited. It takes four years to train a parrot. Order now!

PC-1 . . . . Prices begin at $2,399.86

Altar Server Training Suit

For clergy in charge of training people to serve at the altar, there is often tremendous frustration in teaching all the correct movements and postures. People forget or don't pay attention. What is a concerned liturgist to do? Balmy comes to the rescue with the **BALMY ALTAR SERVER TRAINING SUIT.** This remarkable garment is designed in such a way that attention-getting electrical shocks can be generated by a handheld remote device. Errant movements in the sanctuary can now be controlled. For large churches, consider our Multi-Suit Computer Tracker/ Shocker with the capacity to handle up to six persons simultaneously.

Order No. 21100-S (Single suit & remote) $1,215.33
Order No. 21101-S (Multi-Suit w/computer) $2,990.54

The Balmy Snooze Alert

Clergy work hard preparing sermons. Some spend hours praying, re-searching, and writing draft after draft. Then some members of their congregation have the audacity to fall asleep during the sermon. Balmy Clergy Supply comes to the rescue!

    THE BALMY SNOOZE ALERT is a technological marvel which is easily installed and works flawlessly. The system features very sensitive microphones placed strategically around the church. A frequency filter eliminates all sounds except those in the range of the average snore. When a sleeping person is detected, an alarm sounds in the sanctuary and a high-intensity spotlight shines down on the offender.

    THE BALMY SNOOZE ALERT is guaranteed to cure 90 percent of all snoozers. For the more resistant sleepers, we recommend the optional **BALMY SNOOZE ALERT ELECTRIC GRID INTERFACE.** Embed-ded in pews, the system has the capability of singling out a recalcitrant snoozer and subjecting him/her to 5,000 volts of electricity. This option also may be used to encourage more generous giving during the passing of collection plates.

Order No. 43621-F (Balmy Snooze Alert) $16,213.59
Order No. 43622-F (Electric Grid Interface) $19,483.21

"Fax this list to Santa Claus, e-mail this one to God, and I want to talk direct to Grandma."

© 1996 Doc Goodwin

The message of Christmas is that we should never give up on God. He's raised up drunks from the gutter and opened doors for the frustrated. Look for Him anywhere, but especially in your worst of times. God's message at Christmas is that help is on the way.

—*Rev. John L. Wallace, Presbyterian Church of Sweet Hollow, Melville, New York*

New Year's Scripture: "Behold, all things are become new."
—*2 Corinthians 5:17*

New Year's Thanksgiving: "Thank you, Lord, for fresh starts."
—*Witness,* Bethany Lutheran Church, LaPorte, Indiana

New Year's Toast: "May all your troubles in the coming year be as short as your New Year's resolutions."
—*Irish toast*

New Year's Song: "Ring happy bells across the snow; the year is going, let him go."
—*Alfred Lord Tennyson*

New Year's Reflection: "When you toss out the Christmas tree, be careful you don't throw out the Christmas spirit with it."
—*Rev. Felix A. Lorenz, Jr., Northville, Michigan*

New Year's Prayer: "May the New Year be filled with mirth, music and memories; hope, humor, and health; love, laughter, and lauds."
—*Rev. Brian Cavanaugh, Steubenville, Ohio*

CHAPTER
22

HOLY LAUGHTER *IS* THE BEST MEDICINE

The Church of the Clowns

Holy Trinity Church in London is dedicated to clowns, according to FMC member Bruce "Charlie the Juggling Clown" Johnson, of Kenmore, Washington.

The church has a stained glass window depicting Joseph Grimaldi—father of modern clowning—an altar rail where clowns can kneel and pray, and a clowns' gallery with artifacts from famous clowns. Once a year, clowns from all over the world attend Holy Trinity Church in make-up and costume for a special service, asking God's blessing on all clowns everywhere.

"Holy Trinity is in a section of London described as economically depressed," Charlie says, "and the citizens are pleased that clowns agreed to have their church in an area where laughter is needed the most."

The Clown as Healer

A New York foundation is financing a $150,000 study to find out what the Fellowship of Merry Christians has already demonstrated for the past ten years: that clowns are healers when they visit hospitals.

The year-long project will send thirty-five clowns three times a week into New York children's hospitals to determine if laughter really is the best medicine. Doctors will monitor the results.

A news release announcing the grant declared that the study is believed to be the first to assess "the medical impact of clowns."

Actually, the clowns and health professionals of FMC, Smiles Unlimited of Indianapolis, the Adventures in Caring Foundation of Santa Barbara, California, and other clown ministries to hospitals have been documenting the healing power of the clown for many years.

"Higgins, go in for Carlson."

Adulteration

Joseph Michelli, a staff psychologist at Penrose Hospital in Colorado Springs, Colorado, told the *Gazette Telegraph* that he often uses humor to dispel the fears of patients with cancer or severe depression. His props include clown wigs and juggling scarves.

"Kids laugh 400 times a day. Adults laugh 16 times a day. We lose 384 laughs a day in a process I call adulteration," Michelli said.

—*Gina Bridgeman, Scottsdale, Arizona*

"Are you okay? You hardly slept at all in church today."

Don L. F. Nilsen, professor of English at Arizona State University, in Tempe, is also executive secretary of the International Society for Humor Studies. Professor Nilsen wrote in JN *about the great Protestant physician and theologian Dr. Albert Schweitzer's use of humor as a healing tool:*

Albert Schweitzer was a medical doctor who employed humor not only to combat depression but also to keep from falling into a state of helplessness. Schweitzer once said that disease tended to "leave him rather rapidly because it found so little hospitality inside his body."

Schweitzer found that his use of humor not only helped him deal with stress, but it also seemed to positively affect the people around him. He soon began to realize that the stress involved with illness not only affects the patient, but it extends to the doctors and nurses who take care of these patients as well. He saw humor as being a "vital nourishment" for the hospital community.

Empirical studies conducted by Norman Cousins, Dr. William Fry, and others have shown that humor and hearty laughter can probably affect every system of the body, including the circulatory, respiratory, endocrine, muscle, cerebral, and immune systems.

Humor is important in resolving short-term physical and mental illnesses; however, it is even more important in dealing with long-term disabilities.

A University of Oregon study has found that humor helps marriages last. John and D. J. Rawlings, who have been married for fifty-two years, interviewed seventy couples who had been married an average of nineteen years. Each couple used humor and laughter to avoid conflict or to release tensions.

—*Andy Fisher, New York*

"We'd like to put in a request to lower the pulpit."

Once in a while I read about stress and burnout that are bothering other pastors in other churches. That's not been a problem for me. At Bethlehem Lutheran Church, I think we have found a sure fire cure for any pastor who might have ministerial burnout. We just prescribe a good dose of congregation members who are involved and excited about serving and giving. It works every time.

—*Rev. David P. Buuck, Bethlehem Lutheran Church, Minnetonka, Minnesota*

"Charlie, how did you receive the call to custodial work?"

The secret source of humor itself is not joy but sorrow.
   —*Mark Twain*

The sadnesses of life—far from totally discouraging laughter—gives rise to it.
   —*Steve Allen*

It is far better for man to laugh at life than to lament over it.
   —*Seneca, 4 B.C.–65 A.D.*

A good laugh and a long sleep are the two best cures.
  —*Irish proverb*

Trouble knocked at the door but, hearing laughter, hurried away.
  —*Ben Franklin*

Headache sufferers, it would be cheaper and quicker to listen to a child's laughter than to reach into the medicine cabinet.
  —*Dianna Booher*

Laughter is a tranquilizer with no side effects
  —*Arnold H. Glasow*

If it's sanity you're after, there's no prescription like laughter.
  —*Henry Rutherford Elliott*

FMC member Jeanette Silva of Scott Bar, California, says she wears a button that declares: "WARNING: Humor may be hazardous to your illness."

LAUGH
AND
LIVE LONG

"**H**ardening of the heart makes you grow old faster than hardening of the arteries."

"**W**hen people praise you for your leadership qualities, it means you are starting to resemble George Washington."

"**T**ime may be an excellent healer, but as a beautician, it's not so hot."

"**R**etirement is the time when you never do all those things you said you wanted to do if you only had the time."

"**W**hen you look depressed, people remind you to keep your chins up."

"**O**ld age is a time when you complain that your grown-up children don't visit enough; but when they do visit, you can't wait for them to leave."

"When you're over the hill, you tend to repeat yourself. When you're over the hill, you tend to repeat yourself."

—From FMC member Ron Cichowicz's book **I'm Not Over the Hill**

FMC member Fr. Jim Friedrich of St. Michael's Catholic Church, Herreid, South Dakota, visited an elderly resident in a nursing home, who told the priest he could remember when the old wooden church he attended couldn't get warm in the bitter South Dakota winter. Fr. Friedrich's response: "Many are cold, but few are frozen."

How Old Is Old?

An elephant outlives a monkey,
A turtle, longer than man,
A housefly will last but a summer,
A tree has a long life span.
A camel has humps when a baby,
A deer slows down when fifteen,
Eight years is life's span for a squirrel,
One older is seldom seen.
You are young, my friend, not old but young
If you find deep in your heart
Beautiful thoughts of deeds to be done
Or some kind words to impart.

—Sr. M. Gremma Brunke, Newark, New Jersey
from **Open Sesame,** *reprinted with permission*

On Centenarians

Religion and humor often are important factors in the survival of many centenarians, according to geriatricians who have studied longevity, *Parade* magazine reports.

Frank M. Winn, 101, of Douglasville, Georgia, told the magazine, "I've gone to church since I was nine." Commented Daniel Perry, director of the Alliance for Aging Research in Washington, D.C.: "If people live to 100, how can you think of a person as 'used up' at 65? We're approaching the day when to be 70 or 80 is going to be middle-aged!"

You can't help getting older, but you don't have to get old.
    —*George Burns, at his 95th birthday party*

I try to take one day at a time, but sometimes several days attack me at once.
    —*Ashleigh Brilliant*

The seven ages of man are spills, drills, thrills, bills, ills, pills, and wills.
    —*Richard Needham*

THE THEOLOGY
OF HUMOR
AND JOY

As bass fisherman Harvey Hoops rounds
the bend on a foggy morning, little does he
realize that he's about to enter the *Twilight
Zone* . . .

© 1996 Ed Sullivan

*If Christianity is going to survive all the threats against it, then it is going
to have to respond not only with love but also with joy and wit and
humor. . . . We're not suggesting that the church be a comedy club. But*

The Theology of Humor and Joy   **165**

if our aim is to bring more joy into people's lives, then laughter is just one more expression of joy.

It is the test of a good religion whether you can joke about it.
  —*G. K. Chesterton*

Immediately our religion becomes real; it is possible to have humor in connection with it.
  —*Oswald Chambers*

No one would have been invited to dinner as often as Jesus was unless he was interesting and had a sense of humor.
  —*Charles M. Schultz*

Imagination was given to man to compensate him for what he is not; a sense of humor to console him for what he is.
  —*Francis Bacon*

Humor is another of the soul's weapons in the fight for self-preservation.
  —*Victor Frankl*

If a fellow doesn't have a good time once in a while and get a good laugh out of the serious side of life, he doesn't half live.
  —*Will Rogers*

Laughter is the purest form of our responses to God. Whether or not the great saints were capable of levitation, I have no evidence. I do know that the saints had the power of levity . . . Laughter is the purest form of our response to God's acceptance of us. For when I laugh at myself I accept myself.
  —*H. A. Williams,* Tensions

The head thinks, the hands labor, but it's the heart that laughs!
  —*Liz Curtis Higgs*

There is no surer path to damnation than taking oneself too seriously.
  —*Fr. Francis Randolph, English parish priest in* **Catholic World Report**

The Sioux Indians have a very wise saying: The first thing people say after death is, "Why was I so serious?"
  —*John Tarkov*

"Deadly" is a good adjective to use with "serious"; I've never heard the phrase "deadly humorous."
  —*Lois Grant Palches*

A laugh is worth a hundred groans in any market.
  —*Charles Lamb*

Humor is a proof of faith.
  —*Charles M. Schulz*

Beware of him who hates the laughter of a child.
  —*Lavater*

One laugh of a child will make the holiest day more sacred still.
  —*Robert G. Ingersoll*

Much of what we're about as people of faith is discovering the joy of our relationships to God and each other, and I think humor is an important dimension of who we are as human beings.
  —*Rabbi David Stern, Temple Emanu-El, Dallas, Texas,* **The Dallas Morning News**

In my synagogue, somber is for the dead. My philosophy is that religion ought to be something enjoyable.

—*Rabbi Jack Segal, Beth Yeshurun Synagogue, Houston, Texas,* **The Dallas Morning News**

Jesus had to be able to laugh. When you look at the comics of today, you find most of the greats are Jewish. Jesus dealt with the Jewish people, and they wouldn't have listened to Him if He didn't show humor.

—*Sr. Mary Helen Kelley, Poor Clares Monastery, Memphis, Tennessee,* **Our Sunday Visitor**

God's Gift of Laughter

From Small Wonders, *a book written in 1969 by Rev. Dr. Harold E. Kohn, minister-emeritus of the First Congregational Church, Charlevoix, Michigan:*

While there is much terror and sordid ugliness in the world, there is also a stream of health, cascading like a clear mountain rivulet of melted snow through human experience. This stream is the flow of wholesome, spontaneous laughter—God's gift for refreshing and renewing our souls. A life lived with little laughter is like land devoid of springs, streams, lakes, or ground water; there are some things such a life cannot grow. We cannot take ourselves seriously if we cannot occasionally take ourselves lightly. Laughter is an affirmation of God's final triumph over the worst that can befall us.

After warming up a crowd of several thousand rain-soaked young people with some jokes in the main square of Trent, Italy, Pope John Paul II told them:

"Don't tell your colleagues, and above all the press, that the pope made jokes instead of making a serious meditation on the council . . . Being holy means living in profound communion with the God of joy, having a heart free from sin and from the sadness of the world."

"But enough about me. Where did *your* parents go wrong?"

© 1995 Harley L. Schwadron

God Laughs and Plays

JN *consulting editor Dr. Paul Thigpen, of the Department of Religious Studies at Southwest Missouri State University, Springfield, Missouri, passed on this excerpt from a sermon titled "God Laughs and Plays" by the 14th-century German mystic Meister Eckhart:*

At the least good deed, the least bit of good will, or the least of good desires, all the saints in heaven and on earth rejoice, and together with the angels, their joy is such that all the joy in this world cannot be compared to it. The more exalted a saint is, the greater his joy; but the joy of all of them put together amounts to as little as a bean when compared to the joy of God over good deeds. For truly, God plays and laughs in good deeds.

The Theology of Humor and Joy   **169**

The Grace of Laughter

Charles Honey, religion editor of The Grand Rapids *(Michigan)* Press, *interviewed Rev. John Hitzeroth of Peace Lutheran Church, Sparta, Michigan, about his humorous perspective on life.*

"**W**hen Rev. Hitzeroth looks at himself in the mirror, he figures he's got two choices: laugh or cry. Most mornings, he laughs," wrote Honey.

Hitzeroth told Honey: "Laughter is good for the soul. Being too serious is good for the psychiatrist. When we laugh, we best capture the grace of God. When we get all serious, we get in the way of it."

"Ferguson, did it ever occur to you that I might have a good reason for leaving before the final hymn was finished?"

Comedy is an escape not from truth, but from despair, a narrow escape into faith.

—*Christopher Fry*

Humor is something that thrives between our aspirations and our limitations.
—*Victor Borge*

If you lose the power to laugh, you lose the power to think.
—*Clarence Darrow*

A sense of humor may be the most important thing to wear when you go out in public.
—*Dianna Booher*

Laughter loves company even more than misery loves company.
—*Jim Pelley, Sacramento, California*

An onion makes people cry, but there has never been a vegetable invented to make them laugh.
—*Will Rogers*

Among those whom I like or admire, I can find no common denominator, but among those whom I love, I can—all of them make me laugh.
—*W. H. Auden*

Do not be afraid of laughing a little stupidly and a little superficially. In the right spot this superficiality is deeper than your toiling thoughtfulness. Real laughter, resounding laughter, the kind that makes a person double over and slap his thigh, the kind that brings tears to the eyes, the laughter that accompanies spicy jokes, the laughter that reflects the fact that a human being is no doubt somewhat childlike and childish. We mean the laughter that is not very pensive, the laughter that ceremonious people (passionately keen on their dignity) righteously take amiss in themselves and in others.

God laughs the laughter of the carefree, the confident, the unthreatened. He laughs the laughter of the divine superiority over all the horrible confusion of universal history that is full of blood and torture and insanity and baseness. God laughs. Our God laughs.

—*Fr. Karl Rahner*

If you wish to glimpse inside a human soul and get to know a man, don't bother analyzing his ways of being silent, of talking, of weeping, of seeing how much he is moved by noble ideas; you will get better results if you just watch him laugh. If he laughs well, he's a good man.

—*Feodor Dostoevsky*

President Calvin Coolidge was pretty tight-lipped and never smiled much. Somebody bet me that I couldn't make the President laugh. Well, when we were introduced I said to him: "I'm sorry. I didn't get the name." And by golly, Coolidge laughed.

—*Will Rogers*

I believe we're on earth to delight each other, make each other laugh, and to infuse one another with His joy. Why not? What've we got better to do?

—*Burt Rosenberg, Messianic comedian, Silver Spring, Maryland*

Blessed is the soul that never forgets nor lets go of the Child Jesus. More blessed still that soul which ever meditates on the Grown Jesus. But most blessed is the soul that ever contemplates the Immense Jesus. Scripture says, "The son of Abraham grew and became very great." Isaac means laughter. And so, my brothers, let the Son of God grow in thee, for He is formed in thee. Let Him become immense in thee and from thee, and may He become to thee a great smile and exultation and perfect joy which no man can take from thee.

—*Isaac De LeToile, 12th-century Cistercian monk*

Humor can be a very subversive, revolutionary tool; it's no wonder that in dictatorships comics are the first to be put to death.

—*William Willimon*

Men will confess to treason, murder, arson, false teeth, or a wig, but will not own up to a lack of a sense of humor.
—*Frank Morre Colby*

One nice thing about telling a clean joke is there's a good chance no one's heard it before.
—*Doug Larson*

Humor is today's antidote to hate, fear, and prime causes that trigger hostility and violence.
—*Charles Chaplin*

Laughter can be heard farther than weeping.
—*Yiddish proverb*

The monuments of wit survive the monuments of power.
—*Francis Bacon*

Beatitudes

At a retreat for young people, FMC member Fr. Robert A. Pollauf, SJ, of Sts. Peter & Paul Jesuit Church in Detroit, asked the retreatants to make up their own Beatitudes. Here are the results:

"**H**appy are they who live in the presence of God, for they will never walk alone."

"**B**lessed are they who do not worship the dollar, for heaven cannot be bought."

"**H**appy are they who build bridges among peoples, for they will bring peace to the world."

"**B**lessed are they who die to self, for they shall be filled with God."

"Happy are they who laugh at their own mistakes, for they shall lead merry lives."

"Blessed are the Joyful Noisemakers, for they contribute to the happiness of the world."

The Dance of Joy

Humor historian Paul Thigpen of Springfield, Missouri, discovered this passage in The Little Book of Eternal Wisdom *by the German mystic Heinrich Suso (1366 A.D.). Suso imagines Jesus saying:*

In the Godhead I play the game of bliss,
Such joy the angels find in this,
That unto them a thousand years
But as one little hour appears.
Happy is he who, in joyous security,
Shall take Me by My beautiful hand,
And join in My sweet diversions,
And dance forever the dance of joy,
Amid the ravishing delights
Of the kingdom of heaven.

Hurrah for Pentecost!

What changed Jesus' disciples after the crucifixion from a scattered, frightened band of fugitives into the most remarkable collection of human beings the world has ever seen? What set off the spiritual explosion in Jerusalem at Pentecost?

Thousands of scholars have speculated about that astonishing transformation. Hardly anybody has been able to explain it.

Yet the answer lies plainly in the New Testament for everyone to see. It is found in Luke 24:51-52: "Now it came to pass, while Jesus blessed them, that He was parted from them and carried up into heaven. And they worshipped Him, and returned to Jerusalem with *great joy.*"

Joy imparted by the Holy Spirit was what changed the disciples and knit them together. *Joy* was the first word Jesus spoke when He emerged from the tomb (Matthew 28:9). *Joy* was what Peter preached at Pentecost, quoting the Psalms: "You have made known to me the ways of life; You will make me full of *joy* in Your presence." And *joy* was the atmosphere in the early church as the brothers and sisters broke bread together.

This was not the traditional hushed solemnity that has characterized so much of the church over the centuries. It was euphoria, hilarity, unspeakable gladness. The early believers had become aware, through the outpouring of the Holy Spirit, that the bars of nature had been broken through by their Master's resurrection from the dead.

Recently a young lady wrote to me from Tennessee, "I think Christians ought to be the most joyful people on the face of the earth." Amen!

—JN *consulting editor Sherwood Eliot Wirt*

The Family Circus

"How do you divide your love among four children?"

"I don't divide it. I multiply it."

Reprinted with permission of Bil Keane
from *Behold the Family Circus,* Thomas Nelson Publishers

The Theology of Humor and Joy **175**

Let's build a house of laughter
Where joy sounds from every rafter.
All could there extol,
"Joy's good for the soul!"
For saints here and in the hereafter.
       —Rev. Woody McKay,
         Stone Mountain, Georgia

Joy is the nature of God in my blood.
       —Oswald Chambers

The true expression of Christianity is not a sigh, but a song.
       —Rev. Robert E. Harris, Asheville, North Carolina

Better than beauty and youth are saints and angels, a glad company.
       —Dante Gabriel Rosetti

Angels from friendship gather half their joy.
       —Edward Young

Humor loves company; joy requires it.
       —Janine Katonah, Wichita, Kansas

Joy is the echo of God's life in us.
       —Dom Joseph Marmion

When we live in joy, the virtue of joy, we live in the Kingdom of God.
       —Megan McKenna

The true way to make progress in virtue is to preserve holy joy-ousness.
—*Philip Neri*

We are going to have a feast, a celebration, because this son of mine was dead and has come to life.
—*Luke 15:23–24*

To rejoice is to come back to joy again.
—*Rev. Denny J. Brake, Wake Forest, North Carolina*

Joy and happiness and a knowledge of the Bible will improve your face value.
—*George Goldtrap*

A happy man or woman is a radiant focus of good will, and their entrance into a room is as though another candle has been lighted.
—*Robert Louis Stevenson*

There are some people who have the quality of richness and joy in them and they communicate it to everything they touch. . . . They have such wealth and vital power within them that they give everything interest, dignity, and a warm color.
—*Thomas Wolfe*

All who would win joy must share it. Happiness was born a twin.
—*Lord Byron*

Joy comes not to him who seeks it for himself, but to him who seeks it for other people.
—*H. W. Sylvester*

I don't know what your destiny will be, but one thing I know: The only ones among you who will be really happy are those who will have understood how to serve.
—*Dr. Albert Schweitzer*

It is better to create happiness for others than to pursue or create it ourselves.
—*Lloyd Douglas*

No sacrifice is worth the name unless it is a joy. Sacrifice and a long face go ill together.
—*Mahatma Gandhi*

A sorrow shared is but half a trouble, but a joy that's shared is a joy made double.
—*Msgr. Arthur Tonne*

Better a morsel where contentment is than abundance without joy.
—*The Talmud*

You will never see the stock called Happiness quoted on the Exchange.
—*Henry Van Dyke*

He is the happiest, be he king or peasant, who finds peace in his home.
—*Goethe*

Stop complaining about the management of the universe. Look around for a place to sow a few seeds of happiness.
—*Henry Van Dyke*

No one is a failure in this world who lightens a burden for someone else.

    —Rev. Robert E. Harris

The name of Jesus is honey in the mouth, music to the ear, a cry of gladness in the heart!

    —St. Bernard

Be of good cheer; I have overcome the world.

    —John 16:33

In the Bible, the words "Fear not" can be found 365 times: once for every day of the year.

    —Catherine Hall, Pittsburgh, Pennsylvania

A church should be an oasis of joy and hope in a desert of depression and fear.
> —*Brother Zorba*

He makes our sorrowing spirit sing.
> —*Hymn, "Beautiful Savior," Gesanbuch, Munster (1677)*

The Lord Is the Joy of My Life

The Lord is the joy of my life, I shall never be bored.
He brings me into the fellowship of happy friends.
He gives me ecstatic confidence;
He enchants my soul.
He leads me in the way of jubilance for His own great praise.
Yea though I struggle through the experience of gloom
I will fear no sadness; the joy of the Lord is with me;
Thy grace and Thy cheer, they delight me.
Thou preparest a table before me in the presence of the
    prophets of gloom.
Thou anointest my head with gladness.
My heart bubbles over with joy.
Surely delight and rapture shall follow me all the days of my
    life;
And I shall rejoice in the presence of the Lord always.
> —*Earl Chadwick Carver, Columbia, Pennsylvania*

SURPRISED BY LAUGHTER

"The motion we participate in Unity Sunday passes 6–5."

© 1996 Steve Phelps

JN *consulting editor Dr. Terry Lindvall, president of Regent University, says he is "an ordained Congregational minister, a member of First Presbyterian Church in Virginia Beach, Virginia, attends my wife's First Baptist*

Surprised by Laughter **181**

Church in Norfolk, and has Episcopal leanings." Dr. Lindvall is the author of a delightful book titled Surprised by Laughter: The Comic World of C. S. Lewis *(Thomas Nelson). In the following article, Dr. Lindvall sings the praises of the merry-hearted English Catholic wit, G. K. Chesterton, who greatly influenced C. S. Lewis.*

Almost two decades ago when we were the original faculty members of what was to become Regent University, John Lawing, former cartoonist for *Christianity Today*, took me aside and introduced me to a writer who would smash my stereotypes of Christian writing: G. K. Chesterton.

As a student of C. S. Lewis, I was familiar with Chesterton's name, but immersing myself into his universe, my own sanity was turned topsy-turvy. I got wet with wonder, drenched with delight.

Here was the mystery of God made more marvelous and more mirthful. Where Lewis made me think, Chesterton made me laugh with understanding.

For archaeologists of the comic, the sound of holy laughter in the twentieth century will bear the quirky high peahen pitch of Gilbert Keith Chesterton, journalist extraordinaire and apologist of the grand paradoxical Christian faith.

Few journalists have described their own profession with more accuracy and objectivity.

"Writing badly," wrote Chesterton, "is the definition of journalism." Journalists "cannot announce the happiness of mankind at all . . . they can only represent what is unusual." Chesterton pointed out that newspapers would inform us that Lord James had died when we didn't even know that he had been alive.

Chesterton was the most notable figure on Fleet Street since Dr. Samuel Johnson and would keep a merry company in any public house captive to his wit and humor. But as his fame grew, so did his girth.

"Beware the man whose belly does not move when he laughs," goes the old Chinese proverb. To be within range of the seismic laughter of the man born to be a fifth of a ton, was to be in the realm of divine laughter. There is little doubt that God Himself was the jolly co-conspirator of this doodling saint. Where Chesterton walked, the Lord's earth would quake with gladness.

Chesterton's pilgrimage from youthful agnosticism into Catholic orthodoxy was a festive romp leading to a place where faith and laughter were wedded in holy matrimony. While both wit and humor bubbled out of this high-spirited man, he was aware of their difference, and their proper places in a hierarchy of charity.

His favorite debating adversary was the agnostic playwright George Bernard Shaw.

Wit was a weapon for Shaw. But wit, from the minds of wits like Shaw and Voltaire, could only produce a smile on the lips and not a laugh from the lungs.

"Angels can fly," said Chesterton, "because they take themselves lightly." To be solemn is easy for a person, but laughter requires a leap and a release. "It is much easier to write a good *Times* leading article than a good joke in *Punch*," observed Chesterton.

C. S. Lewis borrowed this thought in his *Screwtape Letters*. For him humor involved "a sense of proportion and a power of seeing yourself from the outside." One needs levity lest one think too highly of oneself. Satan, noted Chesterton, "fell by force of gravity." The devil took himself too seriously and proudly.

Pastor Elton enters Virtual Morality.

© 1996 Jonny Hawkins

Mephistopheles had wit, but no redeeming humor. Falstaff had that humor which keeps company with humility and with all that is common, low, and human. Chesterton championed that kind of honest, earthy humor.

As April Fools' Day approaches, let us ponder Chesterton's observation that "a lunatic is not startling to himself, because he is quite serious; that is what makes him a lunatic," and his remark that "if a man cannot make a fool of himself, we may be quite certain that the effort is superfluous."

As Christians confessing our follies and our fallen nature, we can look at our own hearts and weep and repent; then we discover the grace of God, sit at His banqueting table, and laugh uproariously.

So I am grateful for this laughing saint who has opened my ears to the laughter in the universe. It is he who reminds me that the one majestic secret of the Christian life is joy, and it is the joy and mirth of our Lord Jesus Christ that we are eager to taste at the Marriage of the Lamb.

A Message from the Little Girl Who Couldn't Smile

Dr. Richard W. Bimler, a JN *consulting editor, is president of Wheat Ridge Ministries—"Lutherans seeding new ministries of health and hope in the name of the healing Christ"—in Itasca, Illinois. He is the author of* Angels Can Fly Because They Take Themselves Lightly. *The following article by Dr. Bimler is adapted with permission from an article in* Lutheran Education Journal.

Not long ago, surgeons in the Los Angeles area operated on the face of a seven-year-old girl to repair some nerves so that she could smile. All of her young life, she had been unable to smile because of this condition. . . .

The little girl who couldn't smile has a message for all of us. What must she think of the many adults in this world who have the correct functioning nerves in their faces but who never or rarely use the gift of smiling?

She made me remember the times when I have forgotten to use the gift of smiling with my staff, friends, strangers, and even with members of my own family.

In a sense, the Lord "operated" on all of us when he came into the world. Jesus continues to turn the frowns of life into the smiles of life. He changes our Good Fridays into Easter.

Smiling is just one way to share your faith with others. There is certainly much more to our faith than simply smiling. But smiles are one way to connect with people and allow them to know that the Lord is alive and well in our hearts.

It's an old saying, but it still works: "If you see a person without a smile, give her/him one of yours."

Try this experiment: Take a good look at yourself in the mirror. Practice smiling at yourself in the mirror every day and see how you look to others. Then go out and do it in the world!

Use this smile as you go about your ministries for the next week. Flash it to your friends, to your staff, to your family, and even to that rude driver you encounter on the road.

Smiling is contagious. Let's pray for an epidemic.

Acknowledgments and Permissions

Jokes and anecdotes undergo intriguing transformations as they are retold through the years. The editors of *The Joyful Noiseletter* diligently seek to track down the original source for a joke or anecdote. Original sources, however, are not always easy to discover. For instance, we have heard at least a dozen variations of one anecdote about a minister or a priest or a rabbi, depending on the storyteller, and the storytellers have credited it to a dozen different sources.

When we discovered the original source of a joke, we gave due credit in this book. Otherwise, we acknowledged the person who passed on the item to *The Joyful Noiseletter*. To all of these wonderful folks, we say, again, thank you for sharing with us.

The editors are especially grateful to the sixteen gifted cartoonists who contributed to this book: Dennis Daniel *(Brother Blooper)*, Bill Frauhiger, Doc Goodwin *(Phillip's Flock)*, Johnny Hart *(B.C.)*, Jonny Hawkins, Bil Keane *(The Family Circus)*, Ed Koehler, Karl R. Kraft, Dik LaPine, Steve Phelps, Harley L. Schwadron, Goddard Sherman, Wendell W. Simons, Ed Sullivan, Larry M. White, and M. Larry Zanco.

We thank and salute the following *Joyful Noiseletter* consulting editors for their assistance and permission to reprint the named materials:

Dr. Rich Bimler, president of Wheat Ridge Ministries, Itasca, Illinois, and *Lutheran Education Journal* for permission to reprint "A Message from the Little Girl who Couldn't Smile."

Broadman & Holman Publishers, Nashville, Tennessee, for permission to reprint "A Young Pastor's First Baptismal Service" and several of our favorite jokes, from *A Treasury of Clean Jokes* (© 1986), by the late Baptist humorist Tal Bonham, one of the original *Joyful Noiseletter* consulting editors. (Available through your local bookstore and the catalog of the Fellowship of Merry Christians, P.O. Box 895, Portage, Michigan 49081-0895.)

Chaplain Cy Eberhart of Salem, Oregon, for permission to reprint materials from his audiocassette, "Will Rogers, Live!" and from his research on Will Rogers.

Rev. Dennis R. Fakes of Lindsborg, Kansas, for permission to reprint several jokes from his collection of holy humor.

Andy Fisher, senior writer for NBC's *Today Show,* for his numerous humorous contributions.

Rev. David R. Francoeur, pastor of Christ Episcopal Church, Valdosta, Georgia, for the special Christmas gift suggestions for clergy from the catalog of *Balmy Clergy Supply.*

George and Peggy Goldtrap of Happy Talk Speaking Services, Madison, Tennessee, for their entertaining anecdotes and one-liners.

Humorist/encourager Liz Curtis Higgs of Louisville, Kentucky, and Thomas Nelson Publishers, Nashville, Tennessee, for permission to reprint "All the Days of Her Life" from Liz's book *Only Angels Can Wing It* (© 1995 Liz Curtis Higgs).

Dr. Terry R. Lindvall, president of Regent University, for permission to reprint his article "Surprised by Laughter" about the wit and humor of C. S. Lewis and G. K. Chesterton.

Rev. Paul Lintern, associate pastor at First English Lutheran Church, Mansfield, Ohio, for permission to reprint "Worship Takes Off when Flight Attendants Usher."

Sr. Mary Christelle Macaluso, RSM, a.k.a. "The Fun Nun," of Omaha, Nebraska, for her anecdotes.

Quaker humorist Tom Mullen of Richmond, Indiana, author of numerous books of humor—including *Where Two or Three Are Gathered, Someone Spills the Milk*—for keeping us laughing during the hard times.

Humor historian Paul Thigpen of Springfield, Missouri, for giving us some historical perspective on Christian humor through the centuries.

Msgr. Arthur Tonne of Marion, Kansas, for permission to reprint some of our favorite jokes from his eight volumes of *Jokes Priests Can Tell* books.

Dr. Sherwood Eliot Wirt of Poway, California, author of *The Book of Joy* and *Jesus: Man of Joy,* for his contributions and wise counsel.

We are also most grateful to the following members of the Fellowship of Merry Christians for their contributions to this book:

Don ("Ski") and Ruby ("Tah-Dah") Berkoski of Indianapolis, and the clowns of Smiles Unlimited, a clown ministry to hospitals and prisons.

Ron Cichowicz of Pittsburgh, Pennsylvania, for excerpts on the humor of aging from his book, *I'm Not Over the Hill* and for permission to reprint his article, "God's Last Laugh."

Msgr. Charles Dollen of Poway, California, and *The Priest* for permission to reprint several of his anecdotes from his columns.

Catherine Hall of Pittsburgh, Pennsylvania, for the one-liners she has passed on to *JN*.

Bobby Hart, wife of cartoonist Johnny Hart, for the Palm Sunday *B.C.* cartoon that created such a stir at *The Los Angeles Times*.

Rev. Paul W. Kummer, pastor of Grace Lutheran Church, Destin, Florida, for permission to reprint "What if God Had an Answering Machine?"

Rev. Carl Marks, pastor of United Church of Christ Congregational, Arcade, New York, for permission to reprint "Steward: 'A Keeper of Pigs'?"

Mary Wright McHarris of Knoxville, Tennessee, for the poem "Eve and I."

Fr. Paul Mueller of St. Thomas More University Parish, Bowling Green, Ohio, for permission to reprint "Eat Your Edible Bulletin and Reduce Church Litter."

Rev. Kenneth Pollitz of New Creation Lutheran Church, Ottawa, Ohio, for "Basketball Theology."

Humorist Jim Reed of Cotter, Arkansas, for permission to reprint his anecdotes and one-liners about Sunday fishermen and pastors from his new book, *The Funny Side of Fishing* (© 1996 Jim Reed).

Msgr. Lonnie C. Reyes of St. Julia Catholic Church, Austin, Texas, for "The dog as counselor."

James R. Swanson, editor of *The Pastors Confidential,* Costa Mesa, California, for the prayer in "The Sports Section" and for his "Flat Tithe Plan."

Authors Stan Toler and Mark Hollingsworth and Albury Publishing of Tulsa, Oklahoma, for permission to reprint excerpts from the Toler-Hollingsworth book *You Might Be a Preacher If . . .* (© 1995 Albury Publishing).

Fr. Tom Walsh of Scottsdale, Arizona, for his endless supply of good humor and his pipeline to Erma Bombeck.

Rev. Ronald H. Weinelt of McDonough, Georgia, founder of the Association of Battered Clergy, for his story "Prepare Three Envelopes."

Jeanne and Owen Wells of Florence, Oregon, for "A Bumper Crop" of bumper stickers.

Patty Wooten, R.N., aka "Nancy Nurse," of Davis, California, author of *Compassionate Laughter: Jest for Your Health.*

We also wish to acknowledge and thank the following persons for their contributions:

Eli Cantor of Sarasota, Florida, for permission to reprint excerpts from his book *The Devil's Pi* (© 1941 Eli Cantor).

Max Hall of Cambridge, Massachusetts, for permission to reprint excerpts from his article in *Harvard Magazine* on amusing misprints.

Rev. J. Stephen Hines, pastor of St. Luke Episcopal Church, Asheville, North Carolina, for permission to reprint anecdotes from his book, *Easy on the Alleluias, Harry* (© 1995 J. Stephen Hines).

Author Richard Lederer for several bloopers from essays and exams written by Sunday school students.

Prof. Don L. F. Nilsen of the International Society for Humor Studies, Tempe, Arizona, for "Albert Schweitzer Used Humor to Combat Depression."

Will Pollard, editor of the *Ohio Baptist Messenger,* Columbus, Ohio, for permission to reprint "You may be headed for forced termination if . . ."

Last, but not least, we would like to thank Lenore Person, senior editor of Guideposts Books; Janet Thoma of Janet Thoma Books; and Curtis Lundgren, editorial director of Thomas Nelson, for their encouragement and persistence on both *Holy Humor* and *More Holy Humor;* and Todd Ross and Susan Salmon Trotman at Thomas Nelson for patiently guiding the book through the editorial process so quickly.

Index